TEACH YOURSELF BOOKS

HISTORY OF ENGLAND

'There is a great difficulty in writing a short history of this type when it has so often been done before, and it is also difficult to get the right balance and proportion. This book seems to me very clear and well written and eminently readable. It brings freshness to a familiar topic and is also sound and authoritative. In all, I do not think that it could have been better done.'

Sir John Masterman, O.B.E., M.A.
Provost of Worcester College, Oxford

'. . . the author has contrived to touch on most of the important facts, too, and one can agree that the work could not have been better done.'

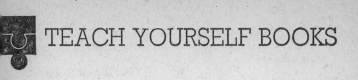

TEACH YOURSELF BOOKS

HISTORY OF ENGLAND

William McElwee

Sometime Junior Lecturer, Liverpool University,
History Tutor, Stowe School
and Director of Modern Subjects,
Royal Military Academy, Sandhurst

ST. PAUL'S HOUSE WARWICK LANE LONDON EC4P 4AH

First printed 1960
Second edition 1970
Third edition 1973
Fourth edition 1974

ISBN 0 340 17885 X

Printed and bound in England
for The English Universities Press Ltd
by Hazell Watson and Viney Ltd, Aylesbury

CONTENTS

CONTENTS

MAPS

GENEALOGICAL TABLES

CHAPTER I

The Roman Conquest and its Permanent Legacy

55 B.C.—A.D. 410

IT is not easy to say when the history of England really begins. From cave dwellings and drawings, flint arrowheads and tools and crude, early pottery, archaeologists can tell us much of the men who inhabited the country for thousands of years before Christ. But for much of that time what is now England was not even an island. There was nothing much to distinguish the Stone Age men who lived this side of the swamp of the North Sea from Stone Age men anywhere else. Only with the coming of the so-called Beaker folk of the Bronze Age, probably soon after 2000 B.C., do we begin to discover some of the influences which shaped England as we know it. The Icknield Way, running down from the Wash over the Chilterns and the Thames to Silchester, commemorates their network of tracks converging on the Salisbury Plain area, where they seem to have been most densely settled, and where still stand the two great stone circles which were their temples at Stonehenge and Avebury. They mined tin in Cornwall and they traded with both Ireland and Europe; and as the bronze age merged imperceptibly into the Iron Age their stock became mingled with that of fresh waves of Celtic immigrants from the east and their level of civilisation began to rise fast. Their axes and sickles and cooking pots began to take on their modern shape. They had wheeled vehicles and probably a crude, shallow plough. Traces of their great fortified camps survive here and there all over central and southern England, and air photographs can pick out on the chalk Downs the pattern of their villages and their little enclosed fields.

The steady movement westwards of one human race after another from the bleak north-east, where most of them seem to have been born, was one of the main factors which shaped this early Britain. Hunger drove them to push steadily westwards their predecessors who had been softened into some degree of civilisation by a kindlier climate; and it was in the extreme west, with their backs to the Atlantic—in Brittany and England, Ireland and Scotland—that the remnants of each accumulated and mingled. This process, continuing on into recorded history, would in due course bring Romans, Saxons, Danes, and Normans to pile up against the last Celtic bastions on the Atlantic.

The other main factor moulding the pattern of all early English development was geographical. The north and west, from Cornwall and Dartmoor up the Welsh Marches and along the Pennine Chain, were high, bleak, and barren, and hard to penetrate. The centre and south, though cut up by dense belts of forest on heavy clay soils and by the great swamps which ran inland for miles from every river mouth, offered large areas of light, chalky ground, easy to cultivate with primitive tools, and a lowland plain where habitation could be dry without being too exposed. Here, inevitably, the new invaders carved out their inheritances, mingling sometimes with the original inhabitants to the great enrichment of their common civilisation, or driving them up into the hills where there already survived innumerable remnants of lost peoples and backward ways of life.

Britain was in the throes of one of these transitions in 55 B.C., when her recorded history really began with the crossing of the Channel by Julius Caesar. The latest batches of invaders—Belgic tribes who were carving out kingdoms west and north of what is now London—brought with them some admixture of German blood, and so added some rudimentary political sense to their native Celtic artistic ability. They had also made some slight contact with Roman civilisation, had learnt to strike gold and silver coins on Roman and Macedonian models, to produce a more finished pottery than any seen before in

ROMAN BRITAIN
The Roads and the Wall

0   20   40   60   Miles

Marsh

Britain, and to make a larger ploughshare which would turn the heavy soils north of the Thames valley. With their continental trading and their close contacts with their tribal kinsmen over in Gaul they began a process of peaceful penetration of Roman fashions and manners which Caesar's two invasions, of 55 and 54 B.C., did not seriously interrupt. For these were really only armed reconnaissances, designed to show that conquest was possible and to discourage the British tribes from assisting their factious kindred in Gaul. For a century civil wars and troubles elsewhere prevented Rome from following up the experiment, while the legendary Cymbeline established a kingdom which covered East Anglia, Essex, Kent, and most of Wessex and which he ruled from Colchester with a quasi-Roman authority for thirty-five years, proudly striking coins as 'Rex Brittonum'. Then, in A.D. 43, the general Aulus Plautius landed with four legions as the advance guard of an annexation which was to be directed by the Emperor Claudius in person.

The Romans wanted British corn and the produce of British mines, and at the same time to stop the ceaseless troubles stirred up in Gaul by the Druid priests of the independent British tribes. Moreover, British disunity made it look as if the conquest would be easy. In fact it did not turn out to be easy or ever really effective. Within eight years Caractacus, heir to Cymbeline's kingdom, had been sent a prisoner to Rome and the frontier had been pushed forward to the newly built Fosse Way, which ran from the legionary base at Lincoln to Cirencester and Bath. Already the great main roads radiated from London north, north-west, and west, along the lines which they follow to this day; and round the more important towns there were growing colonies of veteran soldiers to secure what had been gained. But in the year A.D. 61 the second revolt of Boadicea, the Queen of the Iceni, showed how precarious the achievement was. She destroyed the colonies at Colchester, St. Alban's, and London, and cut to pieces the IX Legion before the Governor could get back from his Welsh campaigning to deal with her. Outside the towns Roman rule, which stood for land-grabbing, conscription, and heavy taxes, remained, and was long to remain, alien and detested.

Moreover, the impetus of the advance died away before the conquest was really complete. Agricola, who was Governor from A.D. 77 to 84, saw clearly that the only logical frontier was the Atlantic and, had he been given the time and means, would even have undertaken the conquest of Ireland. He subdued Wales with a system of roads and forts round Brecon, another road running westward from Chester to a new fort at Caernarvon, and a coastal road linking the two. But he had to leave the conquest of Scotland incomplete. He pushed the frontier forward : first to the fortified line of the Stanegate, from Corbridge to Carlisle, which he linked by road to York and Manchester; and then to the narrow thirty-seven-mile gap, between the firths of Forth and Clyde, which was also temporarily fortified and linked by road to the south. He even marched boldly into the Highlands, won a great battle at Mons Graupius somewhere just north of Perth, and with his fleet subdued the Orkneys. At the same time he launched reforms intended to make the conquest a less skin-deep affair in the already colonised area, extending the system of Roman law-courts to try to bring under control unscrupulous officials and greedy landlords, initiating a large-scale public building programme, and striving to educate the British chieftains and their children in the Roman way of life.

But in the 350 years for which they remained in Britain the Romans could never find the devoted Governors and large numbers of troops and imported officials needed to complete the task along the lines indicated by Agricola, and to make the whole of the British Isles into a genuinely Roman province rather than an imperial garrison outpost. The withdrawal of one regular Legion left only three : the II based on Caerleon-on-Usk, the XX at Chester, and the VI at York. These with auxiliary regiments drawn from every land in the Empire made up a permanent garrison of perhaps 50,000 men—not enough for Agricola's large plans. His Forth–Clyde line was abandoned after thirty years and only reoccupied and refortified once again for a short time in the middle of the 2nd century by the Emperor Antoninus Pius. The Empire's frontier became the great Wall built by the Emperor Hadrian from coast to coast just north of the Stanegate, with a deep ditch behind as a second line of defence, forts and signal posts at every mile, and occasional larger fortresses which would hold a regiment. Its very strength shows how bitter and undying was the hatred of the Pictish tribes of the north; and even then it was not enough. The garrisons were constantly weakened by the drawing off of Legions by pretenders to the Imperial throne in the civil wars which periodically convulsed the Roman world. By the year 200 the last of the outposts north of the Wall had been abandoned for good and at least one barbarian raid had penetrated the defences, ravaging as far south as York and Chester.

The Emperor Severus, an indomitable old man half crippled by gout, had re-established the defensive system by the time he died at York in 211, and it held after that more or less for a century and a half. The first great breakthrough came in 367, when Saxon pirates and Scots from Ireland joined the Picts in a massed assault which swept far into the south. After that it was never properly restored. By 400 the garrisons had been withdrawn from the Wall and from the Welsh forts, and in 407 the last of the regular troops left Britain for good. The thirty-oared boats which poured out of the estuaries of Elbe, Jade, and Rhine loaded with Saxon sea-rovers had, combined with the ceaseless Pictish pressure, broken Roman resistance. The loss of the fleet based on Boulogne, which was taken off by its commander Carausius, in 286, to support his bid for an independent kingdom in Gaul, was never made good, and the strain on the coastal defences became gradually too great. These were re-organised by the Emperor Constantine in the early years of the 4th century, with forts and signal stations all along the coast from the Isle of Wight to the Wash and the II Legion brought across from Caerleon to act as the main reserve, the whole being co-ordinated by a new official significantly named the Count of the Saxon Shore. So long as the Saxon raids remained, like the Pictish and Scottish attacks, mere local incursions, this defensive screen sufficed. Until Constantine's death in 337 only the coastal and frontier areas were periodically devastated, and British wealth and civilisation in the centre and south of the island continued their steady, peaceful growth. After the great massed raid of 367, in which even London was sacked, decay set in everywhere; and when, forty years later, the last of the soldiers and officials went, there was hardly anything left to resist the invaders.

For even in its heyday of peace of prosperity—the 'Blessed Tranquillity' of which Roman coins boasted—Britain was never really absorbed into the Roman world. In the mountains beyond Chester and York and in the south-west there were only military establishments, and perhaps half of the island's million inhabitants lived almost untouched by Roman civilisation. Round the forts and along the Wall were married-quarters and markets for the produce of local farmers and craftsmen, and thousands must have trooped in from afar to fill the great amphitheatre at Caerleon, where a rich township had sprung up round the legionary headquarters. But mostly the tribes lived apart, paying their tribute and finding their quota for the imperial armies, but always aware of lost lands and a legendary independence, regarding the representatives of Rome as aliens and enemies. The luxury of the great villas—large-scale enterprises run on slave labour—which were thrust here and there into the wilderness was envied, but little imitated by their barbarian neighbours. The Bronze Age men lived on in their primitive stone huts or pit dwellings, less in touch with Rome than with the Celtic world beyond the border, whence they drew all the inspiration of their arts and crafts.

Only in the more densely populated south and east did the towns grow from mere garrison and trading posts into genuine civic centres. The villas multiplied along the main roads and up the river valleys; and London, at the junction of all the great roads and with easy access by the Thames estuary to the sea, became a great metropolitan trading port, sending out corn and—already—cloth to

continental markets and bringing in the pottery and
luxury goods from Gaul and the fringes of Germany.
There were *coloniae*, whose inhabitants could claim all
the privileges of Roman citizenship, at Colchester, Lincoln, Gloucester, and York. St. Albans was a flourishing
municipality and Bath already a popular health resort
whose civilisation radiated through thickly grouped villa
estates into the surrounding countryside.

This town culture, with its standard buildings and
institutions, was entirely cosmopolitan. Men scribbled
their wistful sentiments and rude jokes on the walls of
public buildings in Latin and drew their architecture,
their literature, their entertainments, and the gods they
worshipped in their many temples from Rome. Amidst
the mixed population of settlers and merchants and retired soldiers, immigrants from all over the Empire, the
Briton lost all trace of his own racial tradition and became himself a Roman. The larger tribal units—relics of
the kingdoms conquered by Claudius—had a Roman administration superimposed on them; and their capitals,
such as that of the Atrebates at Silchester, which boasted
walls twenty feet high and a forum a hundred yards
square, became Roman provincial towns, aping as nearly
as possible the continental model.

It is not easy to discover by excavation how deeply
this rich cosmopolitan culture penetrated the countryside. Certainly in the villas there was the same high standard of comfortable living. Even the smaller ones, perhaps
no more than large farmhouses and built of wood, were
always centrally heated; and the larger ones were great
stone mansions with every modern convenience, floored
with mosaics and beautifully decorated with wall paintings. These last must have absorbed whatever there had
been of village life, using the original inhabitants as
labourers—perhaps as slaves. They clustered thick wherever climate and soil made country life prosperous and
attractive, in Kent and Hampshire, and in the Isle of
Wight; and there the old tribal life must have disappeared
altogether. But a few miles away, cut off by forest or
marsh from the world of the villas and the towns, it

survived intact for centuries. Even in Somerset, where more than sixty villas have already been identified, there were still in the 4th century villages where men dug themselves pit dwellings and lived exactly as their ancestors had done 500 years before the Romans came. Moreover, even in large areas of the more populous and Romanised part of Britain, in Warwickshire and Norfolk, round York, and down the western borders, this villa civilisation scarcely penetrated at all. There the Ancient Briton remained simply the Ancient Briton, meeting Rome only in the person of the soldier, the official, and the tax collector; resentful of government interference and jealous of a prosperity he did not share or understand; only too ready, if opportunity came, to join the barbarian from outside in a raid on the nearest Roman town or villa.

Thus the Roman civilisation in Britain looked to Rome alone for authority and government, for protection, for inspiration, and for much of its prosperity. For the elaborate town life, buttressed by the export of corn to Italy, was a luxury far beyond the means of the backward local population, of whom only a tiny proportion made any direct contact with it at all. Fifty years before the Legions left—even before the great barbarian raid of 367—the whole fabric was in decay. Under the threat of some local raid or disturbance, villa owners would bury their domestic silver and coins and flee, and would never get back to recover them; and soon the local inhabitants would be quarrying the buildings to make their stone huts. In the towns ambitious housing schemes and public buildings were abandoned half-finished, and soon the poorer citizens there, too, were helping themselves to floors and stonework. Deprived of nourishment and protection from Rome, the provincial life of Britain proved itself to have no roots and no centres of self-reliance. Here and there a Romanised official of exceptional energy and talent might briefly prolong in a small area Roman organisation and discipline. British chieftains, resuming a local and tribal sovereignty, fell to fighting among themselves for the spoils of Rome instead of combining against the new invaders, and the alien, urban civilisation seems almost to have perished of inanition before the barbarian arrived to complete its destruction. The great garrison town of Chester was simply abandoned, to stand derelict until it sheltered a Danish army 500 years later. Similarly the Atrebates, when their tribal existence had no longer any use for a provincial capital, gradually abandoned Silchester. Only the roads and, on the fringes, a native Christian Church, remained as the permanent Roman contribution to English history. All the rest—organisation, language, buildings, culture, and law—perished within a century of the departure of the last Roman soldier.

CHAPTER II

The Saxon Settlement and the Establishment of Christianity
410–800

THE Saxon conquest marked the most obscure period in all English history. What written records there are, whether British or Saxon, were all based on legend and tribal memory long after the event, and often rewritten later as propaganda : to glorify a Saxon dynasty, or establish the claim to pre-eminence of a Welsh bishopric. Sometimes a deposit of Saxon remains on top of the British may help the archaeologist to date the event, but it tells us nothing of the fate of the original inhabitants. Where a settlement was merely abandoned without being reoccupied by the conquerors, we cannot even guess at the disaster which overtook it.

Enough coherent evidence, however, survives to make it clear that Angles and Saxons and Jutes did not immediately move in to fill the vacuum left by the Romans. Most of the remaining structure and civilisation of Roman Britain was destroyed by the British themselves; by local chieftains insufficiently Romanised, or by tribes which poured back from west and north into the country from which they had been driven. Since there was no organised resistance, Saxon raids certainly became more frequent and more devastating. But they remained raids only. Having devastated the countryside the war galleys sailed back with their plunder and their captured slaves to bleak, sandy homelands in Frisia or Schleswig, and it was a Celtic civilisation which first overlaid the Roman, substituting Irish or Welsh pottery and trinkets for the continental models, and a mode of life and government which only very distantly aped that of the Roman officials. The legend is almost certainly basically true which attributes the first regular settlement to Hengist's band of Jutes, called in to Kent by the British prince, Vortigern, to help him in a local feud. By 449 these Jutes had apparently taken permanent possession of the Isle of Thanet, and within another twenty years the whole of Kent had become a Jutish kingdom.

There followed 150 years of haphazard conquest on which no single or simple pattern can be imposed, since conditions in Britain itself already varied so much. When St. Germanus came over from Auxerre in 429 to deal with some local heresies, he found in the south a Christian, provincial Roman world still well enough organised to repel a large-scale barbarian attack. In the north and west Welsh and Pictish chieftains were carving out for themselves principalities which were hardly yet Christianised and in all other respects purely barbaric. The first war bands, arriving without women or cattle, would obviously take over what they could, and the conquest of Kent, for example, was clearly a peaceful penetration which did not involve the extermination of the original inhabitants. What emerged was an Anglo-Saxon kingdom, heathen in religion and with new systems of landownership and government. But the excavated cemeteries and houses of Canterbury show Saxon and Britons peacefully co-existing until, presumably, they merged into a single community. Cut off by the Thames and by the impenetrable Sussex forest which the Saxons called the *Andredsweald*, but easily accessible to continental trade, Kent quickly became a separate kingdom of surprising prosperity.

Farther north along the east coast the Baltic folk whom the chroniclers call the Angles seem often to have followed the Kentish pattern. Britons lived on behind the Roman walls of Lincoln while the newcomers, who did not like town life anyway, gradually filled up the surrounding countryside. Moreover, the invaders preferred to carve their settlements out of the woods wherever they could find good, dry soil in the river valleys, while the Britons had always stuck to the high ground, so that they often existed side by side for considerable periods before the older communities were destroyed or absorbed. Certainly almost all the early invaders took Celtic wives, but often the men, too, were absorbed into the new communities as slaves, or even occasionally as freemen and landowners.

There was no very great or clear distinction between the various invading stocks. East Anglia obviously took its name from the Baltic island which is still called Angeln. A solid block from Jutland colonised Kent and spread from there into the Isle of Wight and Hampshire. Between the two, spreading over southern England and into the Midlands, came the more numerous tribes who actually called themselves Saxons. These differentiated themselves rather by the areas they settled than by their tribal origins. The fighting bands of the legendary King Aella, settled on the South Downs, hemmed in between the *Andresweald* and the sea, became the South Saxons, and their kingdom Sussex. Around London and across the Thames in Surrey were the Middle Saxons, who never achieved a kingdom, but left their name to Middlesex. The East Saxon kingdom of Essex, like Kent isolated by dense forest and easily accessible to Europe, also achieved an early coherence and independence. Other and more numerous bands pushed up from the south coast, along the Thames valley and down the Icknield Way from the Wash to coalesce in Wiltshire, Berkshire, and Hampshire and along the opposite bank of the Thames under another legendary fighting leader, Cerdic, whom the later Kings of Wessex claimed as the founder of their House.

Thus geography, rather than tribal origin, shaped the settlement, penning South and East Saxons and the Men of Kent to the coast behind dense belts of forest and isolating the East Angles of Norfolk and Suffolk beyond the marshes and fens which stretched south of the Wash. The valleys of Trent, Welland, Nen, and Ouse shepherded the MiddleAnglians into the West Midland area which was to be the core of the kingdom of Mercia. The Pennine Chain and the Lincolnshire fens dictated the shape of the other Anglian kingdom of Northumbria, and the pattern of the southern chalk hills grouped the West Saxons round the Salisbury Plain area which had been the heart of Celtic Britain and pushed them westwards through the gaps in the Somerset forests and north-west into the Severn valley.

The early stages of this colonisation were rapid. St. Germanus came back in about 460 to find that the resistance of central England had largely collapsed. Except for Kent, and possibly Sussex, there were as yet no recognisable Saxon states, but the era of settlement had clearly begun. All up the river valleys running in from the Wash and up the Thames and its tributaries the pirate bands were clearing their fields and building their houses, turning themselves into village communities. On the other hand, British resistance was hardening into something less local and sporadic. The Saxons were having to fight hard for every fresh gain, and the fighting was becoming what it had not so far invariably been—a war of extermination. Effective political unity was beyond the capacity of the Celt, but a spreading Christianity was giving the whole western Celtic world a new consciousness of solidarity in face of the heathen. The Christianity of Roman Britain seems never to have rooted deeply and certainly nowhere survived under Saxon conquest. But the founding of the church at Whithorn, in Galloway, by Ninian on his return from Tours in 397 launched a missionary movement which evangelised all Cumbria and Wales, sent Patrick to Ireland, and ultimately brought back from Ireland Columba and his disciples and fellow workers who, between them, were to recover for Christendom great areas of northern barbarism which Rome herself had not yet been able to reach.

In consequence, from about 470 onwards, the Saxon advance was virtually halted for more than fifty years. There was Aurelius Ambrosianus, descended from Roman Emperors, who fought the Saxons to a standstill round Glastonbury and Bath, and there was the more shadowy, though more spectacular figure who has come down as the hero of Celtic legend, Arthur. Little can certainly be said of Arthur save that he unified and inspired British resistance as nobody else ever did and that one of his many unidentified victories was at a place called Mt. Badon, soon after the year 500, and was for the time being recognised by the Saxons as a final defeat. They were stopped roughly on a line running down the Middle of England, and some even seem to have sailed away in search of easier conquests elsewhere.

But after fifty years, during which the Saxon area steadily filled up with fresh immigrants and new settlements, the advance was resumed. The decisive victories were won by two of the larger states which were by now emerging from the jumble of tribes and war bands. At Deorham, near Bath, in 577, Ceawlin of Wessex, Cerdic's great grandson, won a battle which gave him, with Cirencester and Gloucester, control of the mouths of Avon and Severn, and so finally cut Wales from Devon and Cornwall; and at the other end of the frontier, at Chester in 613, Ethelfrith of Northumbria defeated the massed forces of the Welsh princes and massacred after the battle 1,200 monks from the great school at Bangor who had come to pray for victory. "Whether they bear arms or no," he said, "they fight against us when they pray to their God." This second defeat cut the Welsh off also from the Cumbrian Britons, who were soon after to be forced back from the Dee into a small pocket north of the Ribble. The exploitation of these two victories virtually completed the Saxon conquest. Though the Welsh would for long prove invincible in their mountain strongholds, there was no longer any question of a serious counter-offensive.

Meanwhile the pattern of the Heptarchy—the seven kingdoms which were England's first political framework —was beginning to emerge. Ethelfrith's Northumbria, resulting from the union of Deira and Bernicia in 588, now stretched from the Humber to the Forth and across to the Lancashire coast and penned back the Britons into Cumbria, Galloway, and Strathclyde. Norfolk and Suffolk made up the small, politically unimportant kingdom of East Anglia. Geography and commercial prosperity preserved two surprisingly powerful kingdoms in Essex, which included London and Middlesex, and Kent. Along the south coast there was Sussex, isolated and backward, but independent. Finally there sprawled across central England two less well-defined units. Westward from London on both banks of the Thames there was Wessex, weakened after Deorham by quarrels with the Jutes of the Isle of Wight and by a struggle to secure Surrey from the Middle Saxons; and in the Midlands was a jumble of small kingdoms which was to merge during the next century into the Kingdom of Mercia under the Staffordshire dynasty of Penda.

The wars of these shadowy, semi-tribal kingdoms, among themselves or against the Welsh, are not seriously worth recording. It was, however, important that, towards the end of the 6th century, one or other of them began to claim and, indeed, sometimes to exercise, a vague and ill-defined supremacy over the rest, giving their ruler the title of *Bretwalda,* which implied some kind of overlordship. Ethelbert of Kent seems first to have asserted this primacy, but it was lost to Northumbria in 616 in consequence of the great victory at Chester. In the 7th century Mercia produced in succession three exceptionally able kings, Penda, Ethelbald, and Offa, who defeated the Northumbrians, conquered East Anglia, and by 733 had invaded and subdued Wessex. But nothing constructive emerged. There was no fusion of conquered territories, and the rival dynasties survived, waiting their chance. Within a few years of Offa's death in 796 Egbert of Wessex had reversed the process and in turn defeated all his neighbours. But by then this shadowy overlordship was already insignificant; for the first Danish raid in 787 had heralded a fierce struggle in which the Heptarchy was to perish and out of which a real English national monarchy was to be born.

The royal squabbles of these two centuries were unimportant; but the steady growth meanwhile in the Saxon villages of a new pattern of society and a new conception of law and liberty was a decisive influence in shaping later English institutions, and through them has affected the political and social development of most of the modern world. Of equal importance, at least, was the return of Christianity to England from Roman, rather than Celtic

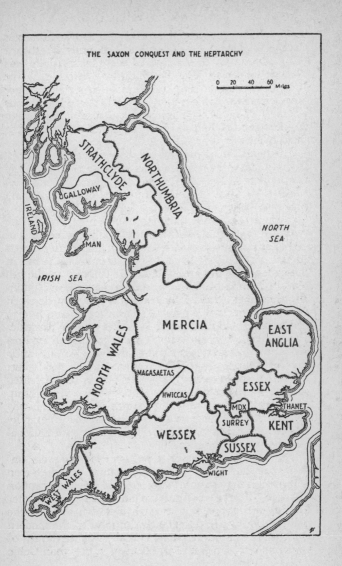

THE SAXON CONQUEST AND THE HEPTARCHY

0 20 40 60
Miles

STRATHCLYDE

NORTHUMBRIA

GALLOWAY

IRELAND

MAN

IRISH SEA

NORTH WALES

MERCIA

MAGASAETAS

HWICCAS

WEST WALES

WESSEX

NORTH SEA

EAST ANGLIA

ESSEX

MDX

SURREY

THANET

KENT

SUSSEX

WIGHT

sources, so that the island's history was again linked directly with the main stream of European culture, this time with more permanent effect.

Saxon villages grew directly out of their war bands and immediately took on many of the same characteristics. They were in the nature of joint-stock enterprises in which every man had freely engaged, had perforce taken his fair share of the risks, and was entitled to his fair share of the winnings. But since the band as a whole took the risks, winnings were also the property of the band, and because any major enterprise had needed the consent of the band as a whole, an element of democratic control was infused into their society from the very start. But this was offset by the inescapable discipline of a piratical venture. The greater authority and responsibility invested in the leaders entitled them to a larger share of gains and a more powerful voice in important decisions.

Saxon society was thus free, but never equal. The centuries in which they had fought their way westwards had given the tribes hereditary nobles and chieftains and a deep respect for kingship and the blood royal, though they would never endanger the whole tribe by accepting the leadership of a baby or a weakling. In such cases a folk moot—a meeting of all the clan, or of its most important representatives, its wise men—would choose the most suitable man of the royal stock, who would then become the leader in war and the dispenser of justice. His absolute authority in a crisis would thus be tempered by the tough self-reliance of the men he led, and he dispensed justice in the presence of all the freemen, or of their representatives who were, in some not very clearly defined way, parties to his decisions. Out of these germs would grow, in the course of centuries, trial by jury and the institution of Parliament.

In accordance with these general principles they parcelled out their settlements among their members, according to their status, as free holdings, though the whole remained Folkland—the property of the tribe as a whole—and must not be given away or sold. Their farming, too, was at first a joint-stock enterprise. Each village cultivated three great open fields, one of which lay fallow each year, and enclosed one large pasture for the use of all. The basic unit was the family; and each family held a number of strips in the common fields, a right to graze a given number of beasts on the common pasture in winter, and a fair share of its hay every summer. In the surrounding, uncleared forest, scrub, and marsh there was pasturage for swine and sometimes additional cattle, and unlimited firewood for all. It was in the meetings of free-men to regulate all these arrangements, in deciding when to close the pasture for hay, in settling disputed rights and allotting such necessities as fresh-water supplies, that the English first began to learn how to govern themselves.

One other important principle was similarly carried over from the war band into the early Saxon legal system. Every community—family, village, tribe, or kingdom—was held jointly responsible for the misdeeds of any of its members; and, since primitive justice was chiefly concerned not with punishment but with exacting compensation for the victims of crime, this largely took the form of assessing corporate fines. When men were few and precious and all life was hazardous, it was more practical not to saddle the community with yet another orphan family by hanging a murderer; and the status of the different ranks of society was marked by the values payable as compensation if they were killed. By the year 700, when things were beginning to settle down, it cost 1,200 shillings or 200 head of cattle to murder a King's Thane, the most important kind of noble, half that amount for a lesser noble or a large landowner, and 200 shillings if the victim was an ordinary freeman. Welshmen, or British survivors where they existed, were reckoned at half-price. Finally there were certainly slaves in all the larger house-holds: descendants of conquered Britons, prisoners of war, or men who had forfeited their birthright of free-dom. But the Saxon never depended on slave labour as the Roman had, and his was essentially a free community.

This, then, was the pattern of the scattered society which the Saxons built up all over England during the first two centuries of their settlement. It was primitive, rough, and barbaric, made by men who had not only fought for their land but had carved their holdings out of intractable forest. To the Saxon poet the land itself seemed hostile, with its black, threatening cliffs, its bleak uplands, and its miles of impassable forest and marsh whence wolves and bears, eagles and ravens would devastate their flocks and robber bands descend on their homesteads. Against such a background it cannot have been easy for Christianity to preach the gentler virtues.

The Christian religion which the Romanised Britons carried back with them into their Welsh fastnesses was a curious tribal affair which was liable to combine the excesses of the primitive Church everywhere with all the characteristic Celtic vices. In remote mountain caves hermits earned a reputation for holiness by a fanatical asceticism reminiscent of early Christianity in Egypt, while the official priesthood—monks grouped in tribal monasteries—simply replaced the exterminated Druids, becoming a hereditary caste endowed with semi-magical powers, corrupt, and too closely indentified with tribe and race to have any possible missionary value. Only a lucky accident renewed the contact with Rome which was essential for expansion or even survival. The Welshman, Patrick, descended from three Christian generations on the borders, was carried off as a slave and brought back when he was freed a new inspiration from Gaul and Rome. The Irish Church which was founded between 432 and his death in 461 became one of the great civilising influences of western Europe. It was still tribal and monastic in organisation, but it had a missionary force which sent out, among many other lesser men, Columban to found monasteries as far afield as Switzerland and Italy, and Columba who, from Iona, won both Picts and the Scots of Argyllshire for Christianity and whose disciples were to convert two-thirds of England.

Columba, one of the most lovable of all the great saints, died at Iona in 597, characteristically in the act of blessing the monastery's old white horse; and in that same year Augustine landed in Kent with forty followers as the spearhead of Pope Gregory's mission to the Saxons. He came as the official protégé of Bertha, King Ethelbert's Frankish and Christian queen, and the royal backing should have given him a fair chance of converting all southern England. But pastorally he was not at first successful. The official world of Kent adopted the new religion with the same perfunctory lethargy as they had shown in worshipping the old heathen gods, and progress in Essex and East Anglia was dishearteningly slow. The greatest success was achieved after his death by the last of his followers, Paulinus, who accompanied a Kentish princess to Northumbria and, rather too easily, won over the whole of that nation, only to see all apparently lost seven years later when Penda, the heathen Mercian, killed the newly converted King Edwin and scattered his supporters.

Out of this disaster came the impetus of the final Christian triumph. Edwin's nephew, Oswald, took refuge in Iona and brought back with him, when he recovered his throne, a new inspiration. From there, too, he summoned Aidan, the first of the great line of teachers and saints who evangelised not only northern England, but in the end Mercia and Wessex as well: Chad, the first Bishop of Lichfield, the great Abbess Hilda of Whitby, Wilfred, Benedict Biscop who gave form and organisation to the work of the evangelists, and Cuthbert, the most saintly and lovable of them all. At the great Synod of Whitby in 663 the assembled Churchmen of the north took perhaps the greatest decision of all. In the teeth of the school of Iona they broke away from the Celtic Church with its different day for Easter and its variant practices, and pledged the allegiance of English Christianity to Rome and the Pope. Penda, the last of the great heathen kings, was dead; and the last organised resistance to the missionaries collapsed. A politic marriage brought in Wessex and, characteristically last of all in its coastal isolation, Sussex.

The effects of all this on the development of England cannot be effectively summarised. In the practical sphere the gains of the preaching saints were consolidated by the great Theodore of Tarsus, a Greek monk sent by the

Pope in 669 to be Archbishop of Canterbury. It was he who mapped out the bishoprics and gave England a system of authority which would prevent a relapse into the tribal, monastic chaos of Wales and Ireland. A proper parish organisation had to be postponed until the piety of rich noblemen had built and endowed churches and permanent homes for their priests. But meanwhile the great centres were so organised that they could reach out with visiting clergy into every corner of the land to baptise and marry and bury their flock. In the monasteries and cathedral schools of the north, and later round Canterbury, there grew up a tradition of piety and learning which astonished Europe. Abbess Hilda's stableboy, Caedmon, became the first great English poet, and the great educational revival which produced at Jarrow as its finest ornament the Venerable Bede, made England for nearly a century the unquestioned leader of Western thought and religion. Her missionaries vied with the Irish in converting the Germans and Dutch, and the works of her scholars were copied for eager readers in every monastery and centre of learning in Europe.

This tremendous development spelt the end of the world of the seven warring kingdoms. It linked England to a great cultural tradition which reduced to insignificance her tribal rivalries and which tamed and civilised some, at any rate, of the fierce Anglo-Saxon virtues. The Church's organisation cut across the frontiers and made of England a single province of Rome, and it placed at the service of any ruler enlightened enough to use it the powerful force for law and order and decency released by Augustine and Columba and their followers. A unified state was an almost inevitable consequence, and Egbert of Wessex, who had lived at the court of Charlemagne and knew more of the art of government than his neighbours, might well have been the man to achieve it. But before he could do so the Danish invasions plunged England into a fresh chaos in which Saxon Church and state all but perished together.

THE HOUSE OF WESSEX

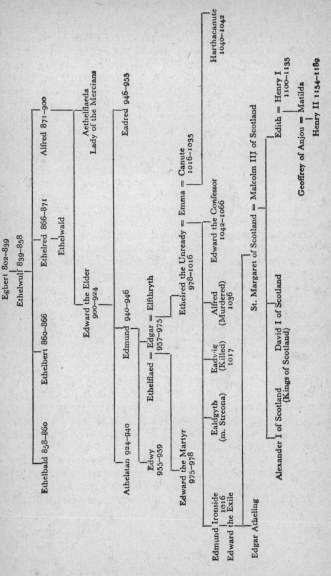

CHAPTER III

England United. The Triumph
of the House of Wessex
800 – 978

THE Vikings who were Christendom's main scourge for
the next two centuries were in almost all respects what the
Saxons themselves had been 400 years before, but writ
large. In everything they seemed a little bigger than life-
size : in their berserk rages and their heathenish devotion
to the old war gods; in the seafaring skill which carried
them to Iceland and the mainland of America, and the
fighting qualities which enabled a few thousand of them
to terrorise not only northern Europe but the Mediterranean, and to establish kingdoms far afield as Naples and
Novgorod; in their enormous, drunken appetites and the
ferocity with which they carved up their captives or sacrificed them as burnt offerings to their gods. Reading the
Christian annals of their doings it is difficult to remember
that they also had their virtues. They had the old, sturdy,
Saxon independence which easily became a love of freedom. Their farming was as energetic as their fighting;
and when they settled down they were great traders,
which the Saxons never were.

They were driven out to piratical adventure from the
same Scandinavian areas as the Saxons, in the same type
of open boat, and by the same forces : the pressures of
other races, of over-population on the scanty Baltic past-
ures between the mountains and the sea, and the thrust
of Charlemagne's expanding power across the Elbe into
northern Germany. Generally they were the landless men,
the younger sons and the outlaws, who must carve out
an inheritance for themselves or starve, with a hard core
of inveterate warriors who had little desire to settle any-

where, but craved only for fighting and plunder, danger, and all kinds of excess. They thus presented a two-fold danger : the raids of scattered bands on all ill-defended coasts and up the navigable rivers; and the more serious threat, when the bands gathered for a great killing, bringing into the field an army of 10,000 men capable of shaking a kingdom to its foundations.

Two main streams of them poured down on the British Isles : the Norsemen proper who mostly came by Orkney and the Hebrides into the western seas and whose main fury fell on Ireland, on the Picts of the north, on Wales, and the coasts of Cumbria and Lancashire; and the Danes who followed the old Saxon lines of invasion up the east- and south-coast rivers. In time they would create model states with first-class military and political organisation. But their immediate impact was traced in the smoking ruins of villages and monasteries which added a new clause to the Church's Litany : "From the fury of the Northmen, Good Lord, deliver us."

When Saxon kings could catch the Danish armies, which were mounted and highly mobile, though they fought on foot, they could usually defeat them. But they could not check the rising toll of sudden raids; and in 851, as a sinister sign of worse to come, the enemy settled down in the Isle of Sheppey for the winter instead of sailing home with their plunder. In 866 the full storm broke. Within four years East Anglia had been annexed and its king martyred at Bury St. Edmunds—whose name commemorates his death—and Northumbria had been overrun. The Mercians had lost all the eastern part of their kingdom and were fighting desperately with their backs to the Severn, and in 871 the whole Danish force was thrown across the Thames in what was intended to be the final assault on the surviving Kingdom of Wessex.

This was one of the great crises of England's history, and it threw up one of her greatest figures. Alfred was the youngest of the four grandsons of the great Egbert, who had been the last to assert the shadowy supremacy of *Bretwalda*, a bookish and physically unimpressive young man of twenty-three, his mother's favourite son, but otherwise unpromising. In 871, when the Danes moved out of their fortified camp at Reading to fight what was undoubtedly intended to be the decisive battle at Ashdown, two of the brothers had already reigned and died, and the third, Ethelred, was on the throne. He was brave enough, but had a streak of ineffectual piety which made him a dangerous ruler for troublous times. At Ashdown, when the Danes were spotted forming up on the high ground, Ethelred was at mass and would not be interrupted, and it was Alfred who deployed the army and led a spectacular uphill charge "like a wild boar," throwing the Danes into such confusion that when Ethelred finished his prayers and came up with the reserves they were totally defeated.

This was the sort of leadership which Saxons needed in a crisis, and throughout that summer, when they fought nine pitched battles and lost most of them, Alfred gave it them. Very early in the campaign Ethelred died, wounded and worn out by hardship. His sons were children and in accordance with the old custom of piratical days the Wessex assembly of wise men—the *Witangemot*—chose Alfred to succeed him. He failed to win the campaign, but he gave the Danes such a fight that in the autumn they willingly let themselves be bought off, some to seek easier conquests elsewhere, the rest to settle down under the greatest of their leaders, Guthrum, in the newly conquered lands of East Anglia and eastern Mercia.

Seven years later the storm broke again. Guthrum concentrated all his forces at Gloucester, and King Hubba, the legendary terror of the Irish seas, gathered in his scattered Norsemen for a descent on Devon. Alfred had used his breathing space to reorganise the Wessex defences, creating a small fleet, and dividing the country levies—the Fyrd in which every able-bodied freeman had to serve—into two, so that half would always be available while the others saw to the harvest. But in 878 these measures had no chance to prove their value, since Guthrum, in breach of all the customs of war, caught the King almost defenceless while celebrating Christmas at Chippenham. Within a few weeks Hubba had pinned the

Devonshire Fyrd against the coast in an old fort at Kenny Castle, and Alfred, with a few hundred Thanes and some hastily collected levies, had taken refuge in a stockade on the isle of Athelney, deep in the almost impenetrable Somerset marshes.

This was the legendary period of Alfred's career, when he is supposed to have burnt the cakes he had been set to watch by a swineherd's wife, and when he certainly did drop a brooch which was found 800 years later and is preserved in Oxford. He was, however, keeping the enemy under close observation from his fortified base and methodically planning his counterstroke. Wessex was already divided into shires for administrative purposes, each with an Ealdorman to mobilise its levies. Odda, the Devon Ealdorman, dealt independently with the western crisis, sallying out and annihilating the superior force which was besieging him at Kenny Castle. Meanwhile Alfred moved out from Athelney in the second week of May, gathered the levies of Somerset, Dorset, Wiltshire, and Hampshire, and fell upon Guthrum at Edington. After a hard fight the Danes were routed, pursued into their fortified camp at Chippenham, blockaded there for a fortnight, and forced to a formal surrender. At the so-called Treaty of Wedmore Guthrum and twenty-nine of his leading men consented to be baptised, and they promised to leave Wessex for ever.

This dramatic victory secured for Alfred all England south and west of the Watling Street, but it was a sadly decayed inheritance. A century of Danish invasions had all but destroyed Saxon civilisation. The Church whose great cathedral schools had taught Greek and Latin, music and astronomy, and had sent out missionaries to reclaim great tracts of Europe from barbarism, could now scarcely muster a priest south of the Thames who could speak Latin. The crafts had perished along with learning and letters, and trade hardly survived at all in seas filled with pirates. All the land, Alfred himself wrote sorrowfully, was "harried and burnt," and his nation was a community of illiterate farmers whose only other and necessary skill was war.

Alfred's quality, unique in history, was that, in spite of a youth spent in almost continuous fighting, he saw beyond the pressing military necessities the vision of a nation restored to piety and learning and the arts of a prosperous civilisation, and worked tirelessly, often single-handed, to achieve it. He did not neglect military security. He fortified towns along his frontiers and round the coast as refuges and centres of resistance to cover the gathering of a field army. Where there was no old town to fortify he built, as at Oxford, a new one; and he garrisoned these new 'burhs' by granting men land on condition that they maintained a house within the town and manned its walls in an emergency. To meet the problem of Danish mobility on sea and land he built a fleet and mounted his greatly enlarged force of King's Thanes who held their land on condition of doing regular military service. Thus he always had a quick-moving, hard-hitting force to pin the enemy down while the Fyrd was gathered in from the shires.

It took longer to restore the elements of civilisation among his backward and barbarous subjects. He had to import teachers, bishops, abbots, and at first even monks from Wales, from relatively undamaged western Mercia, from Germany and France. He had even to learn Latin himself so as to make his own remarkable personal contribution to the re-education of his countrymen: the translation into Anglo-Saxon of Bede's great *Ecclesiastical History*, Orosius' *History of the World*, and selections from Gregory the Great, Boethius, and St. Augustine. That he made of his administrators and fellow-scholars a band of brothers is clear from their affectionate references to each other and to him in their letters and even in the dry preambles of their charters; and all England looked back on his reign as a golden age.

His practical achievement was on the surface small: a monastery at Athelney, a house of canons at Winchester, and a nunnery at Shaftesbury, a court school where all the sons of his Thanes must learn to read and write Anglo-Saxon and the more ambitious were taught some Latin, and some legal reforms to make available speedier and more uniform justice. But it was all carried through in the twelve years which intervened between two great wars and he had to supply all the impetus himself; and out of it English civilisation was reborn. When it is remembered that he also found time to work with his craftsmen, especially the goldsmiths, designed a new type of warship, and invented a primitive candle clock, his total contribution to English history becomes very nearly incredible.

North of the Watling Street, in the Danelaw, Guthrum and his men were meanwhile merging rapidly with the surviving Saxon population with whom, once the religious difference was overcome, they had much in common. A fresh raid by kinsmen from overseas was liable to unsettle them. But they caused no serious trouble, and it was the Great Army from northern Germany which in 892, tested the strength of Alfred's military and naval reforms. These proved extremely efficient. Unable to capture the new burhs and afraid to meet the full strength of Wessex in battle, the Danes marched from Essex to Chester and back without penetrating anywhere, and the quick outflanking movements of their fleet were foiled by the new warships. In 896 they sailed away, taking back the wives and children and cattle which they had brought with them in anticipation of an easy settlement of southern England. The Anglo-Saxon *Chronicle,* another of Alfred's creations for which historians must always be grateful, recorded the defensive success with becoming humility. "By God's mercy," it said, the enemy had not "utterly broken down the English nation."

It was also God's mercy on the English that the House of Wessex, unlike so many ruling families, produced outstanding men for four consecutive generations. Alfred's son and successor, Edward the Elder, lacked his father's charm and wide-ranging cultural interests, but inherited his military and administrative ability. Working with his sister, the remarkable Aethelflaeda, Lady of the Mercians, who governed his northern territories for him, he set himself to recover the Danelaw piecemeal by pushing burhs forward into Danish territory, covering the operation with a field army too formidable to attack, and so securing each year's gains with a string of permanent garrisons. It was a brilliant adaptation of Alfred's purely defensive tactical system for aggression.

Edward's original frontier had been pushed forward at the southern end from the Watling Street to the River Lea, so as to include London; and that fortified town was now launched on its tremendous career of prosperity, thanks largely to the absorption of a large number of the commercially minded Danes. It served now as a useful pivot for the fresh advance which began in 910 and which in ten years recovered all Mercia, Essex, and East Anglia. When the Danes tried a counter-offensive, Edward simply marched into their own homelands and harried them, and when the Great Army intervened, as it did in the Bristol Channel in 913, the local defensive system bequeathed by Alfred proved perfectly capable of preventing any serious penetration. Disheartened by the remorseless advance of the frontier the Danes soon ceased to struggle altogether, and in 920 the Kingdom of Northumbria surrendered without striking a blow.

The Danes had been grouped in 'Jarldoms' each based on the larger towns in their conquered territory, and these Edward and Aethelflaeda turned one by one into shires on the Wessex model, while the new burhs secured the wavering loyalty of the Danish population. It was obviously for some years a precarious achievement, and the submission of Northumbria, where a Viking sub-kingdom survived, really meant nothing at all. But Edward's son, Athelstan, most spectacular of all that remarkable house, quickly sickening of the chaos of tribal warfare in the north, marched in and annexed the lot, thereby provoking all his enemies to combine in a last effort to prevent the unification of England. He defeated them all—Scots and Strathclyde Welsh, and Norsemen from every quarter of the globe—on the northern bank of the Solway, in the epic battle whose memory is preserved in the great song of Brunanburh. By that victory Athelstan became very nearly what he grandiloquently called himself—Emperor of Britain and Lord of all Albion. He had not only established the first real Kingdom of England; he had made it formidable and important throughout Europe.

The gains were still not very securely held when Athelstan died, two years after Brunanburh, in 940, and each of the brothers who succeeded him in only too rapid succession had to fight hard for his inheritance. Edmund faced all the old dangers over again, was forced back to the Watling Street, and had only just recovered the lost ground in 846 when he was killed in a foolish brawl at his own dinner table. Passing over his infant children, as they had with Alfred's nephews, the Witan chose his bookish brother, Eadred, to succeed him, who rose nobly to the occasion in spite of an indigestion so chronic that he could eat no meat, fought off all his Viking neighbours, and finally pacified Northumbria. But when he died, his eldest nephew, Edwy, was still only fifteen and, worse still, was completely in the toils of a scheming widow named Aethelgifu, who planned to marry him to her daughter and through her rule the state. There was all but civil war, but fortunately Edwy died just in time to avert another partition of England, and his brother Edgar reverted to the family pattern. His eighteen-year reign was the Anglo-Saxon golden age, of peace and prosperity and an even-handed justice at home, and abroad such prestige that eight kings did Edgar homage and rowed him across the Dee to church at Chester after his belated coronation in 973, two years before he died.

Another fifty years of peace and ordered government might have made the achievement of the House of Wessex stable and permanent. Much had been done to pacify the Danelaw, whose laws and customs had been harmonised with those of the Saxons in such a way that the Danish freemen emerged with a slight advantage in status. Danes had a fair share of the higher offices, and Northumbria was divided into two great Danish Earldoms. When Edgar died, the Danish half of England did not stir, and there was every sign that the two races were being successfully fused into a single nation. Moreover, a great reform of the Church had produced another vital stabilising influence. The results of Alfred's restoration had been disappointing. The religious houses which sprang up round the cathedrals and the few monasteries which survived the Danish fury were mostly filled with secular canons who lived remarkably secular lives, wearing no habit, often married, ignoring all rules, corrupt and lazy. The parish clergy were no better, and in many villages the priesthood descended from father to son as a hereditary office. The situation was saved by two great men, St. Dunstan at Canterbury and St. Oswald at York, who, deriving their inspiration from the great European reforming movement launched from the Benedictine Abbey of Cluny, started a genuine religious revival throughout England which produced not only a reformed clergy but a mass of pious and charitable societies among laymen in the towns and villages.

But when Edgar died, these reforms were far from complete. Dunstan and Oswald had handled the secular canons with care and tact, since many of them were connected with the most powerful families and, with their property and perquisites and semi-hereditary offices, represented a formidable vested interest. Other bishops were less patient, and wholesale expulsions filled England with aggrieved and powerful men. There was secular danger, too, in the hereditary power and independence of the Earls who had taken the place of the Saxon Ealdormen in the newly conquered shires. The wars had superimposed on the old Saxon pattern of free communities a feudal system which made almost every man dependent in some degree on a lord. In troubled times it was hard to prove a title to a holding, and a man's chance of saving his property from powerful land-grabbers often depended on the number and standing of the 'oath-helpers' whom he could bring to court to support his claim. Since oaths, like wergelds, were valued by rank, the support of a nobleman's oath soon became essential to any small freeholder in difficulties. So there had arisen the convention that the noble who swore to the title was himself the ultimate owner of the land, and the original freeholder became in some sort his vassal, with obligations of service and loyalty in return for the protection afforded him by the great man.

At the same time the old, rigid conception of inalienable Folkland, the property of the community, had become increasingly inconvenient in a complicated society. The desire to endow churches and monasteries, to reward good servants, or to create a new class with special obligations, like Alfred's King's Thanes, led kings and, in due course the larger landowners, to hand over land by charter— Bookland it was called—so that the new occupier was not strictly an owner, but held it on condition of specified services. The Danish wars produced the same result in a different way by making it often impossible for a small farmer to rebuild house and barn and restock his land without help from a powerful neighbour with capital behind him; and the price of such help would be a certain loss of independence. More and more men found it prudent to 'commend' themselves to some magnate in return for help and protection, and villages passed one by one into dependence on a lord. So there grew up a new class of hereditary magnates who could be collectively as dangerous to a weak King as the over-mighty earls of the Danelaw.

Unfortunately, just at this critical moment of change, when one more strong man might have established the King's power for good, the luck of the House of Wessex ran out. Edgar left two sons by different mothers, each of whom had support from factions of the nobility. The elder, Edward, duly succeeded. But three years later, stopping while out hunting for a drink at his stepmother's castle at Corfe, he was dragged from his horse by her Thanes and killed. So the younger succeeded, Ethelred the Unready and perhaps England's most disastrous ruler, at a moment when the Danish raids from overseas were just beginning again.

CHAPTER IV

Downfall of Saxon England
Danes and Normans
978 – 1066

THE ten-year-old Ethelred cannot be held responsible for
the murder of his brother, but that event turned out to
be only too typical both of the man and his reign. He
was a treacherous coward, vain, incompetent, vicious, and
cruel : not only the worst king, but one of the worst men
in English history. The friends he promoted to high office
were gangsters on the make, and to them he transferred
the lands and power of the old territorial families whom
he eliminated by murder or mutilation : men like Aelfric,
who had helped to kill his brother, or Eadric, nicknamed
Streona, the Grasper, whom he married to his sister and
made Earl of Mercia, and whose life was one long succession of murders and betrayals.

Even a stable, solidly united kingdom could scarcely
have survived. Saxon England disintegrated with heart-
breaking rapidity. Dunstan, the one statesman who might
have steered the country through the crisis of renewed
Danish attack, was ousted from power by the King's
mother and her gang and, having joined with Oswald
in crowning the new king, withdrew from politics to sal-
vage what little he could of his ecclesiastical reforms. Only
too often the dispossessed canons and their powerful relations and backers secured the support of the local Ealdorman and drove the new communities out again; and the
disputes between the rival religious parties added one
more element to the general chaos. A world in which the
King would settle a dispute with the Bishop of Rochester
by plundering his lands and beseiging his cathedral was

not one in which any reform, civil or ecclesiastical, could prosper.

Meanwhile for thirty-eight long years the Danes steadily gained ground until only London held out against them. The emergence of new and powerful kings in Norway and Denmark and even, for a brief moment, in Ireland had filled the seas again with outlawed, homeless men, and their attacks followed the old pattern : first ten years of scattered, all-too-successful raids and then, in 991, the combination of the fleets and armies against so easy a prey, and the big invasions. But the uniting of Denmark and Norway into a powerful kingdom under Sweyn Forkbeard did in the end bring a new factor into the situation. For it placed behind the 'Army' of the pirates an organised power capable of attempting a regular conquest rather than a piecemeal settlement, and this was in fact what Sweyn decided in 1013 to do.

By then it was not very difficult. The futility of English resistance is revealed in every indignant sentence of the Anglo-Saxon *Chronicle,* and the gallant sacrifices of the Ealdormen of the old school who gathered their local levies to pin down the enemy were thrown away because the main army never came up to support them. "When the enemy is eastward, then are our forces kept westward," the Chronicler lamented, and when the fleet or army did make contact with the Danes, always "the leaders first began the flight," and the king himself was never there. The plans of the great fleet fitted out in 992 were betrayed to the enemy by Aelfric. In 1009 another destroyed itself in civil war, when a squadron commander named Wulfnoth turned pirate. The demoralised Witan could only suggest a three-day fast and the daily chanting of the 3rd Psalm; worst of all, it enthusiastically endorsed Ethelred's policy of buying off the heaviest attacks with what was called Danegeld : £10,000 worth of silver in 991, £24,000 in 1002, £36,000 in 1007, and £48,000 in 1012. It is not surprising that when Sweyn attacked seriously in 1013 Englishmen would no longer fight.

Ethelred himself had brought Norway and Denmark into the fight by his futile decision to massacre, on St.

Brice's day in 1002, all the Danes he could lay his hands on, including some he had taken into his own bodyguard, when Sweyn's sister had been among the victims. In a series of big raids the Danish King had discovered how feeble England really was, and in 1013 he took it almost unopposed. The Witan voted for him, and even London surrendered when it was learnt that Ethelred, with his last loyal thirty ships and all the plunder he could lay his hands on in Kent, had taken refuge with the Duke of Normandy, whose daughter, Emma, was his Queen.

Sweyn, a drunken barbarian, died two years later and, incredibly, the Witan invited Ethelred back; and when, after two more miserable years, he, too, died, he had again lost everything except London to Sweyn's brutal, but very able son, Canute. Then the miracle for which Anglo-Saxon England waited almost took place. Edmund Ironside, Ethelred's twenty-two-year-old son, dashed down into Wessex, where loyalty to the old dynasty gave him a fighting force large enough to cut to pieces outlying Danish detachments at Penselwood and Sherston. He was able to bring back to the relief of London an army large enough to defeat Canute in pitched battles at Brentford and Otford, and so, by four hard-fought victories reduced the Danish army to what it really was—a large raiding force based on a pirate fleet.

Edmund had shown what Saxons could still do when properly led, and one more victory would probably have sent Canute back to Denmark. But the corruption of thirty years could not be undone in a few months. For decisive victory over the now concentrated Danish army in Essex Edmund had to have Streona's levies from the Midland shires, and in the last great fight at Ashington, Streona served him as he served everyone who ever trusted him, deserting at the start of the battle and leaving the men of Wessex to be cut to pieces. So Edmund could save only half his kingdom when he made peace with Canute in the autumn, and in the end he achieved nothing except to show what might have been done with a tenth of the courage and sacrifice thirty years earlier. For within a few weeks he died, probably poisoned by

Streona or Canute, and the exhausted Witan would not risk another war on behalf of his infant twin sons or his much less able younger brother. It was simpler and less expensive to recognise Canute as King of all England.

Surprisingly enough he turned out to be a very good one. From 1016 to 1035 he gave England settled peace and greatly expanded trade, while a fresh influx of Danish traders into English towns made them more prosperous than ever before. His rise to power in all three of his kingdoms had been marked by the murder of rivals and the slaughter or mutilation of hostages, and his first acts as king were unpromising : an unprecedentedly large levy of Danegeld and the execution of a number of Saxon magnates. He hounded down and killed Edmund's brother, Eadwig, and sent his infant sons off to King Olaf of Sweden with a message that it would be well if they did not survive. Since the two sons of Ethelred and Emma were out of reach of poison in Normandy, he then struck a cynical bargain with the widow, and the two were married on the understanding that any children either of them had to date should be disinherited.

But Canute was not a brutish drunkard like his father and he was, nominally at least, a Christian. He also knew that he could not in the long run rule England without the goodwill of his Saxon subjects. So he used Danegeld to pay off his Danish army and send it home, keeping only a small bodyguard and a few ships permanently manned. The magnates he executed were those, including Streona, who had betrayed one or both sides in the war; and Edmund's most loyal supporters found themselves in high favour, so that the old Wessex policy of a careful balance of Saxons and Danes in high office was maintained. The result was a reign which has come down in history almost as a golden age. His early brutalities—and, indeed, his later murder of his brother-in-law in a quarrel over a game of chess—have been overlooked, and the pious chroniclers record only the foundation of churches and shrines, the pilgrimage to Rome of 1027 which he cleverly used to get better terms for English trade in continental markets, the peace and prosperity and the good justice he kept. Even the best-known legend, of his rebuke to his courtiers by the seashore, clearly enshrines the tradition of a wise and humble—even a well-loved—King.

Yet all these gains were once again all but swallowed up in a fresh outburst of anarchy on his death. There were too many possible successors: Emma's son, Harthacanute, and his own two elder sons disinherited by his marriage treaty, Sweyn and Harold Harefoot; Ethelred's sons, Alfred and Edward, over in Normandy, and Edmund Ironside's twins far away in Hungary, where the saintly Olaf had sent them to be out of Canute's reach. In the first scramble for the throne, Alfred was captured, blinded, and left to die among the monks at Ely, and Harold Harefoot reigned for five years, dying in 1040 just as Harthacanute landed, accompanied by Emma and his other half-brother, Edward, to assert his claims. But he lasted only for two years, dying, as he had lived, in the midst of a debauch, leaving Edward, known as the Confessor, as the only available heir. So, for a last, brief spell the House of Wessex again governed in what was left of Saxon England.

Canute's sons had been drunken louts. Edward had absorbed from finicky Norman clerics an effeminate civilisation which equally unfitted him as an English king. He took vows of chastity and kept them even after his marriage, and only in Church affairs would he show any energy or enthusiasm: over questions of liturgy, or the building of his Abbey Church at Westminster which gradually obsessed him to the exclusion of all else. He had the white hair and soft, pink complexion of old age long before he reached what should have been his prime, and his dignity was a purely ceremonial thing which carried with it none of the qualities of leadership. The Norman influence he brought with him was resented, and he himself was despised.

The power and wealth of the great Earls, already a problem in Edgar's reign, had become a disruptive menace under Ethelred. By 1042 it was concentrated largely in a single family. Godwin, son of that Wulfnoth who had wrecked the naval campaign of 1009 by turning pirate,

ENGLAND ON THE EVE OF THE CONQUEST

Godwin's Family
Leofric's Family
Siward's Family

0 20 40 60 Miles

SCOTLAND

NORTH
SEA

NORTHUMBRIA
(Morcar)

IRISH SEA

MERCIA
(Edwin)

EAST ANGLIA
(Gyrth)

WALES

NORTHAMPTON
SHIRE

EAST ANGLIA
(Leofwine)

WESSEX
(Harold)

ENGLISH CHANNEL

had made himself Earl of Wessex by a series of treacherous, but well-timed changes of allegiance; and though it was he who had captured and blinded Edward's brother, he was now too powerful to be removed. His daughter had the barren honour of becoming Edward's Queen; his eldest son, Sweyn, had an earldom of his own in the south-west; Harold, the second and most able, was Earl of an enlarged East Anglia. Neither Leofric, who had the bulk of Mercia, nor Siward of Northumbria could challenge so over-mighty a territorial power, and against it Edward was relatively powerless. Only in the Church was he able to promote his favourite Normans, and that on sufferance.

In the dreary round of bickerings among the earls which followed there was little ultimately worth recording. In the end Sweyn went too far even for Saxon England by abducting the lovely Abbess of Leominster, and public opinion forced the whole family into exile in 1051. There was a brief year of Norman triumph at Court, and Duke William came over from Normandy to spy out the land, extracting from Edward, it would seem, some sort of promise to name him as his successor, which, though legally meaningless, would be useful for propaganda purposes later. Then, in 1052, Godwin fought his way back, only to die a year later, leaving Harold for the next fourteen years as the only effective ruler of England. There is little doubt that Harold, too, was already scheming for the crown. He himself took over Wessex, dividing East Angia between two brothers and putting a nephew into Sweyn's old western earldom. But in trying to extend the family power northwards he fatally weakened it. Edwin, Leofric's grandson, fought off an attempt to dispossess him of Mercia and when another of Harold's brothers, Tostig, supplanted Siward's son Waltheof, in Northumbria he quickly made himself so unpopular that the Northumbrians drove him out and forced Harold to give them in exchange Edwin's brother, Morcar. So the whole of the north passed into the hands of two men whom Harold could never wholly trust and who would never trust him. Moreover, Tostig never forgave his brother for not insisting on his restoration and went off to intrigue with Harold Hardrada of Norway who, as a descendant of Canute, had designs himself on the English throne and a slightly better claim than either Harold or William of Normandy.

It was thus on a very lonely and dangerous adventure that Harold embarked when Edward at last died in January 1066. An unfortunate accident had given William more useful propaganda when Harold had been blown ashore on the Normandy coast and forced to promise support for William's claims before he could get away. A Norman invasion could thus be represented as a pious crusade against the 'oath-breaker'—a view which the Pope was prepared to back enthusiastically, since Harold had just forced a schismatic cleric named Stigand into the Archbishopric of Canterbury in the teeth of Roman and Norman opposition. Edward's long illness, too, had given William plenty of time to create a favourable diplomatic situation. He was on excellent terms with the King of France and all his most powerful neighbours had agreed to come in with him on a profit-sharing basis. Far in the north Harold Hardrada and Tostig were arming for an invasion of their own, and Harold's isolation was complete.

So Saxon England faced the last great crisis of its history. Commercially it had become a prize well worth fighting for. Thanks to Canute's trade treaties and the great influx of Danes, London's river bank was now crowded thick with wharves and warehouses which handled a growing export trade in raw wool and the products of English craftsmanship in exchange for Rhineland wine and Flemish cloth. Aethelflaed's burh of Chester had grown from a fortified outpost into a flourishing town on the proceeds of Irish trade, and York grew steadily in wealth and population as the distributing centre of the goods which flowed in from Scandinavia through the north-eastern ports. Local industries were making local prosperity : the iron foundries on the fringes of the Sussex Weald, Worcestershire salt mines, a growing fishing industry on the east coast, and the age-old tin and copper workings in Cornwall and the north. Primitive, once self-supporting village units could now often find a market town where a surplus of some specialised product could be exchanged for the more rudimentary amenities of civilisation; and the growing use of money instead of barter —a process much accelerated by the heavy taxation for Danegelds—was steadily increasing the volume of trade, and so raising standards of living all round.

In contrast the machinery of government was out of date. The old, tidy grouping of villages into hundreds and hundreds into shires, each with its own court of justice, had under the pressure of war become chaotic. At the shire courts twice a year the thanes and reeves and village deputations still met the earl and bishop to transact county business, but below all was confusion. The slow ruin of the old village freeholder begun in the first wave of Danish invasion had been completed in the second; and the intolerable burden of Danegeld had been the last straw. All sorts of private courts and jurisdictions had grown up round the larger estates, to which their neighbours now owed suit and service in infinite variety in return for protection and assistance in a crisis; and these cut across, though they did not always supersede, the jurisdiction of the old free courts. There were wide differences of status and custom, too, between the old Saxon and Danish areas. Men owed service for different holdings in different courts, and kings had added to the confusion in their efforts to protect revenues and authority from the encroachments of local magnates, to turn the produce of the royal manors into a regular cash income, to found a monastery, or to meet a sudden crisis from overseas.

The military organisation was equally obsolete. The society of peasant farmers on which Alfred had based his system had largely disappeared, but the Fyrd remained unchanged. Too much control of the county levies had passed into the hands of the great earls, without whose goodwill the King could hardly raise an army. Absorbed in fighting each other, Saxons and Danes had remained unaware of the evolution of the mounted fighting man and of the archer, and their tactics and weapons were out of date. They depended still on their great, two-handed axes and on their shield wall, used horses for movement only, and still used javelins and throwing-spears instead of bows and arrows.

The progressive impetus behind Saxon society was, in fact, largely spent. Dunstan's Church reforms were still not complete, and vested interests and entrenched abuses everywhere survived. Ecclesiastical appointments were too much at the mercy of the King or of local magnates, so that the Church was secular-minded and over-dependent on the state. Learned and pious bishops, like Wulfstan of Worcester, were exceptions. Stigand, with his train of Thanes, his great hunting expeditions, and his political preoccupations, was the predominant type. In learning, in piety, in its organisation and in its buildings, the Saxon Church lagged far behind its continental brethren, typifying in this the whole of Saxon society.

Only another Alfred or some fresh stimulus from without could have prevented this England from relapsing into the feudal confusion which was to hamper all German development for the next five centuries; and Harold was no Alfred. In thirteen years, when he had virtually ruled the state, he had remedied no abuses and brought none of the decaying institutions up to date. It was his fault as much as anyone's that in 1066 he faced invasion from two quarters with an obsolete and inadequate administrative and military machine, in diplomatic isolation, and at the head of a nation divided in its loyalties. England might have rallied patriotically behind the grandson of Edmund Ironside, Edgar Atheling, a fifteen-year-old boy whom the Confessor had fetched back from Hungary, but Harold had persuaded the Witan to pass him over on the grounds of his youth, quoting the acceptance of Canute as a precedent for taking a king from outside the royal house. But it was a dangerous argument; if Canute and Harold, why not Hardrada, or William of Normandy?

The threat from the north was actually less formidable than it seemed. Hardrada was a giant of a man famous as a fighter as far afield as Constantinople and Novgorod, who had commanded the Emperor's guards and won a Russian princess as his wife; and the army which disembarked from his 300 ships in September 1066 was probably the largest the Norsemen had ever concentrated against England in the 300 years of their intermittent attacks. But it was no more than that : the sort of large-scale raid which the Saxons had repeatedly defeated when properly led. It was chiefly the fact that it coincided with the Norman attack that made it formidable.

William's preparations were a very different affair. Normans were indeed only Norsemen who had been settled in France for little more than a century, but they had shown all the astonishing adaptability of their race. In three generations they had not merely assimilated all that was best in French civilisation, but had improved on it. Normandy was everything Saxon England was not : efficient, tidy, and up to date. The tenants-in-chief held feudal baronies roughtly equal in size with clearly defined legal and military responsibilities attached to them; and the same was true down the scale, through the sub-tenants and lords of manors to the peasant, who was a serf tied to the soil, with settled and uniform obligations and rights inseparable from his holding. From the manor upwards to the Duke every lord had his own law court for his dependants and was entitled to certain fixed grants and aids on such occasions as the marriage of his son or the tenant's own death. Church fiefs had to produce groups of five armed knights like the rest, and a parallel chain of courts controlled Church affairs. All authority in Church or state culminated in the Duke's supreme court, which reserved to itself all cases involving breaches of the peace, licences to build castles, and the like; and the Duke called the councils which governed his Church and, subject to a very remote Papal control, appointed his bishops. In 1034 William had succeeded, as a boy of seven and a bastard, to a duchy in a state of feudal disorder. By 1066 he was not only one of the toughest fighting men in Europe but probably exercised more real power within his dominions than any other living ruler.

Harold's gamble thus started with all the chances

against it. Though feverishly energetic, he could not make up in a few months the deficiencies of years. In May, before his fleet was at sea, Tostig descended on the south coast while he himself was in the north trying to shore up the doubtful loyalty of Edwin and Morcar by marrying their sister. Tostig was repulsed, but merely retired to the Forth to await Hardrada and his promised army; and a long summer of waiting, with the fleet off the Isle of Wight and the Fyrd deployed all along the south coast, put the worst possible strain on territorial levies with their minds on haymaking and harvest at home. By 1st September the fleet was forced to put in to London to provision and refit. On the 12th William began the concentration of his 300 ships and 12,000 men at St. Valéry-en-Caux, and on the 15th Tostig and Hardrada sailed into the Humber.

Rightly or wrongly, Harold dashed north at once with all the levies he could lay his hands on, leaving the south coast protected only by the northerly wind which had brought the Norsemen down from Scotland. He had indeed little choice, for only spectacular personal success could justify to England his seizure of power. In nine days he was at York with his 3,000 housecarles—his personal bodyguard—and such midland troops as he could gather on the way. Passing through the city at dawn on the 25th, he caught the Norsemen completely by surprise at Stamford Bridge, where they had been leisurely celebrating their defeat of Edwin and Morcar five days before. One day's hard fighting settled the northern crisis. By evening Tostig and Harold Hardrada were dead and the remnant of their army could only man 24 out of the original 300 ships to sail away. But it was Saxon England's last day of glory. The wind had changed, and Harold was still at York on 2nd October when the news reached him that William had landed unopposed at Pevensey.

Though in essence only another Norse raid, William's was a much better equipped and provisioned force than Hardrada's, containing most of the best fighting material in northern Europe. Harold did not throw anything like the full fighting force of England against them, for he still dared not give men time to hesitate and calculate the risk of backing his last and most dangerous gamble. He was at London again in five days, leaving the slowly gathering midland troops far behind. There he waited only four days to gather in his own Wessex Thanes, his brothers' forces from East Anglia, and such of the Fyrd of the southern counties as could be got together in the time. On 11th October he moved again, and on the 13th burst out of the Weald on to the high ground north of Hastings, where a ridge protected by dense forests on either flank gave him a position ideally suited to his antiquated tactics.

William, clearly thinking, as Harold did, that delay would disintegrate rather than stiffen Saxon loyalty and courage, had been waiting for nearly a month. For both of them a single battle was likely to settle the issue, and William moved forward so eagerly that his attack, at nine in the morning on the 14th, caught the Saxons before their deployment was complete. Even so, in spite of their tactical advantage and of the fact that half Harold's armly were poorly armed county levies, the Normans battered away at the ridge in vain for more than six hours, unable to penetrate the shield wall and suffering fearful losses from the great axes of the Thanes and housecarles massed round Harold's standards in the centre. The Breton contingent broke and fled, William himself had three horses killed under him, and once he had to ride the length of his line unhelmeted to stop a panic rumour that he was dead. But at three in the afternoon, remembering how once during the morning a Saxon detachment had rashly pursued his beaten troops down the hill and been cut to pieces by his cavalry, he ordered a much larger, deliberately feigned flight. This time so many of the untrained Saxons fell into the trap that the flanks of the ridge could no longer be held. Even then it was not until darkness was falling that the ring of shields and swinging axes in the centre broke at last, worn down by a dropping fire of arrows to which the Saxons had no answer. Harold was hit in the eye and mortally wounded; and the Thanes and housecarles, true to their ancient tradition, stayed and died to a man around him. "In the English ranks," wrote William of Poitiers, William's chaplain, "the only movement was the dropping of the dead; the living stood motionless." So, not without glory, the story of Saxon England came to an end.

THE NORMANS AND ANGEVINS

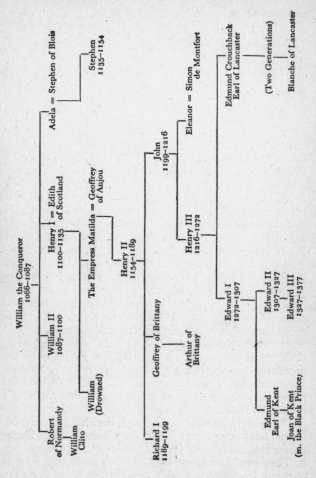

CHAPTER V

Mediaeval England
The Normans and Angevins
1066 – 1327

WILLIAM had been right in staking everything on a single battle. With Harold gone, there was no will to resist, and, as the Normans marched in a wide, ravaging sweep round London, Edwin and Morcar drew prudently off and the dithering Witan sent Edgar Atheling at the head of a deputation to offer the Conqueror the Crown. This not only gave him a better title to the throne than pure conquest, but also enabled him to confiscate the property of almost all the great landowners of south and eastern England as rebels who had fought against him and parcel it out among his followers. The conquest did not quite end with William's coronation. As soon as he returned to Normandy in 1067 there were scattered outbreaks in the west and in Northumbria as the great earls realised the consequences of their selfish hesitation a year before. But they were too late. On each of them William wreaked a fierce revenge, devastating the north from the Humber to the Tees so thoroughly that the vale of York was scarcely populated for centuries. As a result of fresh forfeitures, almost all the cultivated land in England had by 1070 passed into alien hands and the country had suffered not merely a change of ruler but a social revolution.

The orderly Norman mind found the chaos of differing status, land-tenure, and jurisdiction in the Saxon villages intolerable, and manor by manor proceeded to reorganise it. They would recognise henceforward only three classes of men : freeholders, villeins, and cottars. The freeholder could sell or transfer his land as he pleased, though he must commend himself to some lord of his own choosing and pay rent or service for the protection he received. Villeins, who formed the overwhelming majority of the peasantry, normally farmed thirty strips each in the common field and worked three days a week, and some extra days at busy times, on the demesne of the manorial lord. The cottar had only five strips in addition to his cottage and garden, but worked only one day a week for his lord and could hire himself out as a labourer for the rest.

From the information collected by William's clerks and put together in the great Domesday Survey at the end of his reign it is clear that the conquest imposed considerable hardship and loss of freedom on most of the Saxon population. Only one-eighth of them remained free, and those mostly in the old Danish areas. All who had made any surrender of independence at any time were downgraded to villeins to fit them into the rigid Norman system. Only one manor in a hundred remained in Saxon hands, and the only direct beneficiaries were the slaves, who were all classed as cottars to make their status tolerable to the Norman Churchmen.

But in spite of this wholesale reorganisation, England never conformed to the mathematical precision of the Norman ideal. Only on the frontiers, where an almost standing military force was needed to keep out Scottish and Welsh raids, were there compact earldoms on the continental pattern. Elsewhere, thanks partly to the piece-meal nature of the conquest, partly to the Conqueror's deliberate intention of making rebellion difficult, tenants-in-chief had manors scattered through the length of England. Moreover, since he had a free hand in dividing the spoils, William could insist that the privileges and rank attaching to a tenant-in-chief went with the land and descended only to the eldest son, so that England avoided that plague of younger sons who claimed the privileges of nobility without its responsibilities which became such an unmitigated nuisance elsewhere in Europe.

In practice the Norman system was less harsh and less destructive of the Saxon tradition of local self-government than it appeared on paper. The invaders were a tiny minority who could not survive without the goodwill of the peasantry. The manorial lord depended for life and living on sturdy-minded villeins accustomed for centuries to declare the custom of their own villages, and who still did so in his court, though he was theoretically the judge. Even Domesday was compiled on the basis of the sworn evidence of such men, and the manor had to adapt itself to the village, which was more deeply rooted and which would survive it. Moreover, the Shire courts remained, cutting across the ordered hierarchy of feudal jurisdictions, preserving and extending local variations of custom until what emerged in the end was a system neither Norman nor Saxon, but peculiarly English. In the course of time the conquerors learnt as much as the conquered, and between them they made a nation.

Beside these fundamental changes, events on the surface of history under the first Norman kings were of trivial importance. In a rudimentary society the chief business of a king was to maintain order and he was judged by the quality of the justice he enforced, especially against local tyrannies, which were as liable to occur among Norman barons as among Saxon earls. The conquest once complete, there were no great events in the Conqueror's reign. He suppressed baronial rebellions on both sides of the Channel with harsh efficiency, and so the Saxon chronicler, still writing away up at Peterborough, when he had finished listing the people's grievances, added the significant afterthought : "The good peace that he made in the land is not to be forgotten." Suffering was inevitable in a period of rapid change, yet Norman rule, harsh but equitable, was in many ways preferable to the chronic disorders of later Saxon days. The Tower which was rising above London and the feudal castles about the country stood for something more than merely alien tyranny.

William I died in 1087, leaving Normany to his eldest son, Robert, and England to the second, the redheaded William Rufus; and when Rufus was shot, either by accident or murder, while hunting in the New Forest in 1100, Robert was away on Crusade, so that the third brother, Henry, was able to seize both England and Normandy and to hold both until his death in 1135. Through both reigns the pattern remained the same. There were baronial rebellions which tried to play Robert off against his brothers and were effectually suppressed. William II was an ungainly, squat figure without dignity or charm, ill-tempered and immoral, and most harsh in his enforcement of forest law in the vast enclosures reserved for his hunting. Henry I was the best educated of his family and far the most treacherous and cruel. It was he who instituted drawing and quartering as the punishment for traitors, and he put out the eyes of a poet who had lampooned him. But both, surprisingly enough, were popular with the masses, and for the same reason : they "kept good justice".

This popularity emerged with surprising clarity. There was, of course, a basic unity between king and barons who had to stick together lest both become the prey of the conquered Saxons, and the more intelligent barons never pushed opposition to the Crown so far as to endanger the structure of the society they were jointly creating. But there was also a basic struggle between a king who sought to extend his power and his law into every corner of the land and barons jealously guarding their local privileges and immunities. There was also the baron who was purely conscienceless—an anti-social gangster like Robert of Bellême who starved his prisoners to death or watched them roast over a slow fire, or Geoffrey de Mandeville who made life hell for the inhabitants of the Fenlands in the anarchy which followed Henry I's death. But whatever the dispute, the common people were quite articulately on the King's side. Rufus turned out the Fyrd against the baronial rebels in 1088; and when he allowed them to march unscathed out of Rochester, where he had trapped them, his troops shouted for halters for the traitors. Henry took the Fyrd across to Normandy to defeat Robert at Tenchebrai in 1106; and his republication of Alfred's laws and his marriage to Edith, the niece of Edgar Atheling, were deliberate appeals to popular opinion.

Meanwhile, Henry I had begun that steady enlargement of the authority of the Crown which became one of the most permanent and valuable factors in English progress for the next 600 years. Taxation and justice could only be organised in scattered, primitive communities feudally, by delegating all power and responsibility to the local landowner. But, as in Saxon England, this often led to local tyrannies and private wars, and to dangerous diversities of law and custom. National progress depended on the King's ability to thrust into every corner of his kingdom a uniform system of law which would protect the weak from the strong, the poor from the rich. Educational progress, especially in mathematics, enabled Bishop Roger of Salisbury to introduce into the Exchequer the first regular system of accounts and records, and every year two of the King's Barons of the Exchequer toured the country supervising the work of the Sheriffs and their Shire Courts. Their prime duty of ensuring the proper administration of the King's justice has been carried on by the Judges of Assize from that day to this. But originally they had the general duty of supervising the whole business of local government, and through Shire and Hundred Courts they soon began to cut away the power of the local lord and his feudal court.

At the same time the grant of charters to the larger towns began to set traders free from the clogging restrictions imposed by the local manorial courts; the compulsory use of the lord's mill and bakehouse and the multitude of tolls and dues designed for a rural community. Towns expanded rapidly, and so did the volume of trade both inside England and with Europe. London, already a self-governing community, led the way, boasting a hundred churches within its walls and the cherished privileges of electing its own sheriff and paying an annual lump sum in place of the old vexatious taxes and fines. Exports of cloth and wool were still expanding, and the first coal from Newcastle was reaching France to offset the growing import of French wine. Thus, within two generations, the Normans had conferred solid benefits on the English to compensate them for the loss of the old haphazard Saxon ways.

Meanwhile fifteen great new cathedrals symbolised a wholesale reform of the Church which not even a sentimentalist could regret. Archbishop Lanfranc, who had taken Stigand's place at the Conquest, had patiently completed Dunstan's work, letting the married clergy—a large majority—keep their wives, but forbidding any further clerical marriages. The quality of the higher clergy was improved, largely by men imported from abroad who brought with them the standards of a reformed Papacy. New monasteries were founded and old ones like Glastonbury lavishly re-endowed; and bishops, withdrawn from the Shire Courts, acquired their own courts in which they enforced on all clergy and for all ecclesiastical offences the canon law which Rome was steadily spreading throughout Christendom.

In this last development there were, however, the seeds of future troubles. The saintly but obstinate Anselm, who followed Lanfranc at Canterbury, refused to allow William II and Henry I to appoint their own bishops and invest them with the symbols of their office, as the Conqueror had done; and he was so outspoken about the dissolute extravagances of Rufus that he had to leave the country. Under Henry I these quarrels were patched up. English bishops were elected henceforward by their chapters and invested with ring, staff, and mitre by the Church, but compelled to do homage to the King for their 'temporalities'. This sensible compromise lasted, but there were other disputes pending, and a great trial of strength between Church and King was sooner or later inevitable.

The first three Norman kings had thus laid the foundations of a new England, but their achievement was all but lost again in the confusion which followed Henry's death in 1135. His son, William, heir to both Norman and Saxon houses, was unfortunately drowned in the White Ship through the carelessness of a drunken pilot, and his sister, the widowed Empress Matilda, could not command the loyalty of the barons in that unfeminist age. So the Great Council which had grown out of the old Witan, chose instead of her Stephen of Blois, grown son of the old Conqueror's daughter, Adela. Unfortunately Stephen was not a strong enough man to justify this reversion to Saxon precedent: "A mild man and a good," the chronicler said, "and did no justice." With the help of Scotland and some of the barons, Matilda was able to keep an intermittent civil war going for all the "nineteen long winters" of Stephen's reign, and even for a short time established herself as 'Lady of England'. But she, too, like Stephen, quarrelled with the Church, and with her own most powerful supporters; and in 1148 she was driven out again. Five years later her son, Henry of Anjou, invaded the country again and forced Stephen to recognise him as his heir; and a year after that, in 1154, Stephen at last died.

The disasters of the "nineteen long winters" must not be exaggerated. The *Chronicle* was written at Peterborough, in the heart of that fen country where Geoffrey de Mandeville was having men "hanged up by the thumbs" with "burning things hung on to their feet", and imprisoning them in dungeons filled with snakes and toads. But there is plenty of evidence that elsewhere progress continued uninterrupted, in spite of Stephen's inability to control his barons. Great churches were completed at Norwich and Ramsey and Bury St. Edmunds, and so was the famous Winchester Hospital of St. Cross. Exchequer and Treasury clerks still compiled their records, and Assize Judges still toured many of the shires. The mints were turning out good coins, and nothing seems to have disturbed the historical researches of Walter of Malmesbury, or the scientific and linguistic studies of Adelard of Bath. Nevertheless, however local and intermittent the atrocities which drove men to say that "Christ slept and his saints", a strong king was necessary if all this progress was to be maintained. In spite of Stephen, the Normans had rescued Saxon England from the excesses of its own feudalism. It remained now for Henry II and his Plantagenet descendants to secure their gains.

Henry II brought a new dynasty to the throne. But besides the flaming red hair, flaming temper, and restless energy of his Anjou forefathers he had inherited his grandfather's brains, and he was extremely well educated. He also had behind him the power, wealth, and prestige of vast possessions in France, half of which he governed in his own name or that of his wife, Eleanor of Aquitaine, so that no baronial opposition could stand against him. Thus the ground lost under Stephen was quickly regained : illegal private castles were pulled down, new feudal jurisdictions were abolished, and the authority of Sheriff and Shire Court reasserted, while the tours of the Assize judges became more frequent, more regular, and more effective.

Much more important, however, was Henry II's creative work, for which he looked for inspiration not so much to his grandfather as to the Anglo-Saxon past. Out of the custom of taking sworn testimony from the freemen assembled in Shire or Hundred Court he evolved the grand jury : the twelve "legal men from each Hundred" and the four from each village who had to appear at Assizes to declare under oath that true bills had been found against accused persons. It would be another fifty years before the verdict of a petty jury superseded the primitive ordeal by fire or water at the actual trial. But very soon juries began to settle civil disputes instead of the unfair Norman trial by battle which enabled a tough fighting man to treat his neighbours as he pleased, and especially to grab their land on a trumped-up legal case. At the same time there was a steady transference of all important lawsuits into the King's courts, where a man would not be at his lord's mercy. An elaborate system of writs, often devised by the King himself in the restless evening conferences with his ministers which followed a hard day's hunting, enabled every freeman, by application to the King's Chancellor, to force his feudal superior to do him justice. Before long all cases involving murder, arson, robbery, or forgery were withdrawn from feudal jurisdiction altogether, and the quicker, fairer justice available brought more and more litigation before the King's judges. Only the manorial courts held their own against this competition, and they, of course, still handled all the affairs of three-quarters of the population—the villeins who were bound to the manor. But it would not be long before villeins began to free themselves and so to step into all the rights guaranteed to every freeman by Henry's reforms.

These were probably the most important advances ever achieved in English history. Trial by jury has been the greatest of safeguards against governmental tyranny; and out of the oaths sworn by the assembled freemen grew the Common Law of England—an accumulated mass of rights and immemorial customs which protected an Englishman in life, limb, and property, not only against his feudal superior, but ultimately against the King himself. Henceforth all policy for the maintenance of peace and order and of royal authority would have to be formulated within the framework of the common law, and the royal authority itself would come to be identified with the rule of law.

Henry was not a peaceable man. His wife left him in the end because she could not bear his hatreds and the rages in which he would roll on the floor chewing the rushes and screaming blasphemies and abuse; and he quarrelled with all his sons as soon as they were grown up. It was, indeed, rage which killed him when, in 1189, he learnt that his favourite youngest son, John, had joined the combine of his brothers against him. But the quarrels were mostly confined to France. In England, once he had established his authority and cleared the Scots out of the northern shires, he kept as good a peace as any of his predecessors, and would have come down in history with an unblemished reputation if his wicked temper had not involved him in the murder of Archbishop Thomas Becket.

The Church's claim that "criminous clerks"—churchmen, that is, who had committed crimes—could only be tried in ecclesiastical courts was bound to lead to serious trouble. Canon law penalties, even for major crimes, were slight, and the Church insisted that even minor officials, vergers, sextons, and choristers, were clerics and outside the King's justice. So in the first ten years of Henry's reign over a hundred murderers went almost unpunished, condemned only to short spells of imprisonment, or to fasting on bread and water and repeating daily the seven penitential psalms; and public opinion supported the King's demand that such men should merely be unfrocked by the Church and then handed over to his courts for a proper trial.

It was not so easy to find a working compromise on this issue as it had been over investitures, and anyway Henry clearly had no intention of compromising when he appointed Becket, his Chancellor and most trusted friend, to be Archbishop of Canterbury. He was understandably angry when Becket took an obstinate stand on the principle that no man could be tried twice for the same offence, and before long both men were using every petty weapon of annoyance and persecution that came to hand, so that a mountain of misunderstanding overlaid the original dispute. Thus neither can really be said to have been in the right when, in 1170, Becket goaded Henry into his most celebrated explosion of rage, in which he demanded if none of the dastards who fed daily at his expense would rid him of a "turbulent priest". He was probably as horrified as anybody when FitzUrse and three other knights took him at his exact word and murdered the Archbishop on the steps of his own high altar. But public opinion, scarcely aware of the complicated issues and knowing nothing of Becket's provocations, saw only a noble Churchman martyred for his faith by royal gangsters. Becket became England's most popular saint and Henry, swearing his innocence, had to let the Canterbury monks scourge him publicly for his intemperate rage. His main battle was irretrievably lost, and it would be another three hundred and fifty years before another Henry challenged the Church's immunity from the law of the land. History followed the lead of contemporary opinion, and Henry's immensely valuable contribution to the development of English institutions has ever since been overshadowed by that grim scene in Canterbury Cathedral.

The next three reigns demonstrated the soundness of Henry's building. Richard I, the Lion-hearted, was an able soldier who captured the English imagination and has come down in history as a hero, though he spent only ten months of his ten-year reign in England. Vast sums were raised for the army which he took on the Third Crusade to help the princes of Christendom try to recover the Kingdom of Jerusalem from the Saracens, and further vast sums for his ransom when he was captured by one of his enemies on the way home. But neither the expense nor the heavy loss of English lives in Palestine impaired Richard's popularity. Archbishop Hubert Walter governed the land in his absence extremely well, and the main effects of the Crusade in England were the ruin or death of some of the more dangerously powerful barons and a golden opportunity for many towns to buy their freedom by equipping a detachment for the King's army.

By contrast John, who succeeded his brother in 1199, has come down rather more deservedly as one of the great villains of English history. He showed a touch of the family military genius, but all attempts to whitewash him break down before the facts. He lost all his French inheritance and exhausted England with vexatious taxation. He murdered his own nephew and alienated every reputable baronial family. He quarrelled with the Pope on issues which commanded considerable support in the country, but had not the personal popularity needed to win the struggle and in the end abjectly surrendered to Rome greater rights of interference in English affairs than ever before. His viciousness, his treachery, his arbitrary disregard of the law, and his failures made him hated by all, and when in 1215 he faced the baronial revolt, inevitable after fifteen years of misgovernment, nobody would fight for him. For the only time in English history the people were on the side of the barons and against the King.

Magna Carta, the Great Charter which the barons then forced John to sign on the island of Runnymede, was chiefly designed to remedy abuses of feudal taxation which directly concerned only the wealthier classes, and because of this its importance has been belittled. It was, however, very important that the conservatism of the Charter did not look back beyond the reforms of Henry II, so that it bound barons as well as King to a subordination to the common law which the feudal magnates would have indignantly rejected fifty years earlier. Moreover, in defining baronial claims to liberty, it inevitably made statements applicable to all free men, who were henceforth guaranteed against punishment without fair trial, against delay of justice, and against taxation without the consent of "the common council of the realm". There were minor clauses, too, which gave it a less baronial flavour, protecting the privileges of towns and merchants, and stipulating that a villein should never be deprived of his tools. Most important of all, there would come a time when all Englishmen were free to claim the rights asserted at Runnymede only for a privileged few, and when the "common council of the realm" had grown from a gathering of feudal magnates into a Parliament. Whatever the intentions of its authors, the Charter became the foundation of English laws and liberty, and the frequency with which it was confirmed in following centuries sufficiently proves its growing importance.

But for his gluttony, John would probably have defeated the barons in 1216 and annulled the Charter, for they mismanaged their campaign and made the fatal mistake of bringing over French help, so forfeiting their claim to be the patriotic party. John, however, consoling himself for the loss of his army's baggage in the tides of the Wash, gorged himself to death at Newark on peaches and cream, and the more moderate barons were able to expel the French and give England a temporary respite from misgovernment by setting up a regency for John's nine-year-old son, Henry III. Unfortunately the young man grew up not, indeed, vicious like his father, but every bit as capricious, childish, and incompetent. His subservience to the Pope cost England as much in taxation as John's unsuccessful wars, and he squandered further large sums, partly in rebuilding Westminster Abbey, but mostly in personal extravagance and in such wildcat schemes as an attempt to put his younger son on the throne of Sicily. His friends and ministers were worthless foreigners; his policies irresponsible.

The result was another and even more important baronial revolt in 1258, led by Simon de Montfort, Earl of Leicester and brother-in-law to the King, and once again conservative in intention. The foreigners who had filled the Household and governed England over the heads of the regular officials were expelled, the Charter was confirmed, and the King was compelled to accept the assistance and advice of that Council of the Realm which had replaced the old Witan. But Henry brokes his promises and forced a civil war in which he was defeated and captured at the Battle of Lewes in 1264. De Montfort established what was virtually a military tyranny, and it was to broaden the basis of his power and strengthen himself against baronial rivals that in 1265 he took his famous step of calling into the Great Council, which men were beginning to call a Parliament, not only knights from every shire, who had often been summoned before, but two representatives from each of the larger cities and boroughs. He was only really applying the representative principle underlying the Shire Moot; and out of it the House of Commons would ultimately grow. For the moment, however, it was a failure. Henry's very able son, Edward, escaped from captivity, gathered together all the malcontents among the barons, and caught and killed de Montfort at Evesham. Thenceforward, though Henry reigned until 1272, it was Edward who ruled; and the declared basis of his policy was the Charter, the old laws of Henry II, and a properly constituted Council of Englishmen.

Edward I was primarily a soldier and in temperament harshly autocratic, but he saw the importance of a favourable public opinion, and revived de Montfort's method of ensuring it by calling in representatives of all concerned in major decisions and taxation, on no regular system, but so frequently as to make such consultation a permanent feature in English constitutional life. At the same time he first restored and then greatly extended the decayed administrative machine of Henry II. He used Inquests into the conduct of sheriffs, coroners, and even judges to purge out a lot of minor corruption, resumed the attack on private jurisdictions in a new series of writs, and called in Parliament to help him to resist the encroaching power of both Church and barons. He thus picked up all the threads left by his predecessors, and the early part of his reign was a period of great promise and growing prosperity.

Unfortunately, however, all was ruined by his determination to govern not merely England, but Great Britain. He completed the conquest of Wales without much difficulty by 1284, saving the last remnants of Welsh pride by giving them his own eldest son as their Prince. But his attempt to maintain a puppet king on the throne of Scotland and so pave the way to a peaceful annexation broke down, and in 1295 he was forced to start a war which he found he could not win. Though his archers and mounted knights could always defeat the Scottish spearmen if they were properly handled, like Agricola and Athelstan before him he was baffled by the inaccessibility of the Highlands. First under Sir William Wallace and then, after his capture and execution, under Robert Bruce, the Scots fought back heroically, and Edward had still not subdued them when he died in 1307 on his way north for a last attempt. By then England was all but bankrupt, her prosperity had evaporated under heavy taxation, and many of the old abuses had crept back into the administration. There was only one compensation. To finance the war Edward had been forced to rely on even larger and more representative Parliaments and to concede the all-important principle that "what touches all should be debated by all". Thus the 'Model' Parliament of 1295, which became the pattern for all future Parliaments, comes down in history as the greatest achievement of Edward's reign.

The decline begun in the last ten years of Edward I's reign was completed in the next twenty by his son. Edward II was a big, lazy, vacuous man, interested in almost every craft except that of government which, like Henry III, he left to foreign favourites, of whom the most notorious was the Gascon, Piers Gaveston. The attempt to conquer Scotland came to an end in 1314 with the spectacular defeat of Bannockburn, when Edward allowed the finest army England had ever turned out to be caught by Robert Bruce on marshy ground where there was no room to deploy and was totally routed. At home the greater barons, exasperated by misgovernment and goaded beyond bearing by Gaveston's talent for inventing wounding nicknames for them, had already banded together as the 'Lords Ordainers' to try to substitute a better government, but they were never strong enough to get permanent control. In 1311 Lancaster and Warwick, "the Play Actor" and "the Black Dog of Arden", caught and killed Gaveston, and in 1319 Edward revenged him by beheading Lancaster without a trial in the courtyard of his own castle at Pontefract. After ten years of this sort of sporadic civil war Edward had forfeited the loyalty and sympathy of everybody, and his wife, Isabella, and her lover, Roger Mortimer, had little difficulty in taking him prisoner and setting up a regency of their own in the name of his son, another Edward. But though they secured themselves against a restoration of Edward II by having him murdered at Berkeley Castle in 1327, the Queen and Mortimer did not last long, either. In 1330 young Edward III suddenly arrested them both in Nottingham Castle, shut his mother up for life, and sent Mortimer up to London to be hanged on the thieves' gallows at Tyburn, thereby inaugurating what most Englishmen of the Middle Ages would have considered the most glorious of Plantagenet reigns, though by the end of it their monarchy was almost certainly doomed.

YORK AND LANCASTER. THE END OF THE PLANTAGENETS

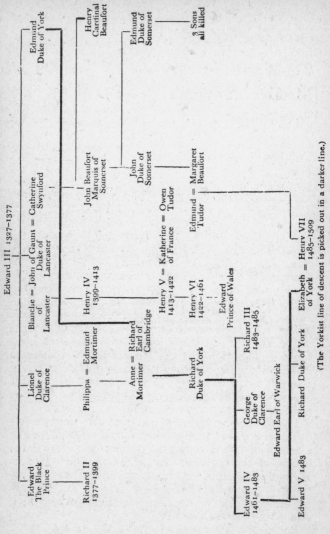

Edward III 1327-1377

Edward The Black Prince — Lionel Duke of Clarence — Blanche = John of Gaunt = Catherine Swynford Duke of Lancaster — Edmund Duke of York

Richard II 1377-1399

Philippa = Edmund Mortimer

Anne = Richard Earl of Cambridge

Henry IV 1399-1413 — John Beaufort Marquis of Somerset — Henry Cardinal Beaufort

Henry V = Katherine of France = Owen Tudor

John Duke of Somerset — Edmund Duke of Somerset

Henry VI 1422-1461 — Edmund Tudor = Margaret Beaufort — 3 Sons all killed

Richard Duke of York

Edward Prince of Wales

George Duke of Clarence — Richard III 1483-1485

Edward Earl of Warwick

Edward IV 1461-1483 — Richard Duke of York — Elizabeth of York = Henry VII 1485-1509

Edward V 1483

(The Yorkist line of descent is picked out in a darker line.)

CHAPTER VI

The Breakdown of Mediaeval England
1327 – 1485

THE French wars of Edward III and his son, the Black Prince, which began in 1338 and lasted, off and on, for over a hundred years, have been invested with a good deal of false romanticism and glory. The two were, of course, quite genuine products of the age of chivalry, by which the Church sought to divert to the defence of the weak or of Christendom the lust for fighting of the mediaeval baron. They were polished and charming to their own class. The Prince waited personally on King John of France after he had captured him in the great victory of Poitiers; and it was not a wholly unworthy conception of knightly honour which made Edward hold back his reserves at Crecy in 1346 to give his son the chance worthily to win his spurs. Even the Order of the Garter was founded in the first place to cover a lady's embarrassment. Moreover these victories, and Agincourt in the following century, gave England the patriotic legends out of which emerged a new nation in which the last distinctions between Norman and Saxon were swept away; for they were not really knightly victories at all, but triumphs of the ordinary English archer, whose quick and accurate fire broke the power of heavily armed feudal cavalry for good. There were sound economic motives, too, behind the flourish of chivalry. The capture of Calais gave London an invaluable depot for the export of wool, and the expanding trade with Flanders and Gascony made it easy for Edward to get all the money he needed from Parliament for so popular a war.

But in the long run the war was ruinous and brutal.

Edward plunged France into a hundred years of misery for the sake of a crown to which he had no shadow of right, and would ruthlessly have hanged the burghers of Calais but for his wife's intervention. The Black Prince burnt Limoges in a fit of temper with every man, woman and child penned inside, and he only turned to fight at Poitiers in 1356 to save his plunder. The Treaty of Bretigny in 1360, which brought England all south-western France, seemed a glorious triumph for the new, self-conscious nationalism, but in reality decline had already set in. A fearful visitation of the bubonic plague, which men called the Black Death, in 1348 destroyed half the population in two years and left England too weak to hold her conquests. Ruinous war taxation was beginning to cripple trade. The Black Prince died and the King sank slowly into senility; and a top-heavy feudal system was beginning to produce over-mighty barons, dangerously inured to war, who would turn on each other as soon as they were released from fighting overseas.

Fortunately before this Edward had rounded off the structure of the Angevin monarchy by bringing the King's justice down from the shire court into every parish. Each county now had its Justices of the Peace—an unpaid local magistracy drawn from among the lesser landowners which dealt in petty sessions with felonies, trespass, and all minor offences, regulated wages, and fixed maximum prices. Moreover, this new squirearchy, closely linked with another rising class, the richer town merchants, had been able to exploit Edward's constant need for money in Parliament, where the shire and borough representatives had formed the habit of withdrawing apart to consider the voting of taxes and so laid the foundations of the House of Commons. Parliament indeed had greatly increased its influence in national affairs, and the King wisely co-operated in this, having all the greatest measures of his reign embodied as Acts of Parliament : the Statutes of Provisors and Praemunire designed to restrict the encroaching power of the Papacy, and the Treasons' Act which gave the subject new safeguards against arbitrary arrest and imprisonment.

All this progress, however, important as it was in the perspective of history, was overshadowed for contemporaries by the immeasurable disaster of the Black Death. The mute evidence of numberless parish churches, grandiosely planned, but left uncompleted when suddenly there were no more masons and no money for building, still underlines the magnitude of that social catastrophe. The plague probably struck hardest at the congested populations of the towns, and certainly the monasteries' losses were appalling : half the monks of Westminster, and forty-seven out of sixty at St. Albans. But it was easier to gear town life down to a shrunken population and recover prosperity as it expanded again. It was on the villages that the blow fell hardest, where every man's individual labour was important to the community as a whole. Often corn remained uncut, and women had to help in what little ploughing there was. Some smaller villages were abandoned altogether, and everywhere the traditional way of life was permanently dislocated.

Hitherto a steadily expanding population had been cutting fresh fields out of the surrounding waste; labour had been cheap and land scarce. Now the situation was reversed. There were too few to till the land, and those who were free to sell their labour for money were better off than villeins tied to their customary week-work. There were plenty of people, too, to help an escaped villein to conceal himself for a year and a day and so become legally free : rival landlords desperately short of labour, master craftsmen in need of apprentices, and merchants without servants. The flight of the more enterprising, the young and the unmarried, made things worse, and the Statute of Labourers, which tried to save landlords from ruin by fixing wages at the 1347 level and imposing hideous penalties on the escaped villein, was quite ineffectual. In the end manorial lords had to face facts and get out of their difficulties as best they could. Some gave up arable farming altogether and enclosed the domain for sheep, which needed much less labour. Others commuted the weekly labour dues for money wages. Others again found that this made their labour bill too high and leased the domain out in small farms for cash rents; and soon the common fields, too, began to be cut up into compact, rent-paying holdings. For a time the villein's status remained unchanged; he was still tied to the village soil and paid his dues to the manor court. But soon the need for fluid labour and the shortage of cash would lead to the abolition of these as well, either by sale or by default. Within a century villeinage disappeared altogether, and with it the manorial court. The peasant, though only a tenant, became a free man, entitled to all the rights and safeguards which neither Henry II nor the authors of Magna Carta had ever intended for him.

Naturally such a social revolution entailed much disorder. The lords fought hard for their dues and rights, backed up by special law courts which, by Edward III's death in 1377, had already sentenced over 9,000 recalcitrant labourers. Peasant exasperation at the attempt to keep them in servitude found an echo in the towns among workers who were being deprived of the protection of guild rules by a rising capitalist class eager to exploit new wealth, and everywhere there was a profound intellectual and spiritual unrest. The richer survivors of the Black Death reacted violently from their panic into an orgy of extravagance and ostentation which showed up the struggles and grievances of the poor even more harshly.

At the same time the Church, which should have given a lead back to sanity, could not even reform herself. The Pope had become a puppet of the French king at Avignon. The richer bishops and abbots went the same way as the laity, and there was nobody to check the relapse of monasteries into inefficiency and sloth. Many monks had private apartments and wore ordinary clothes; parishes were staffed largely by half-educated, poverty-stricken vicars; and a riff-raff of friars and pardoners battened on the superstitions of the common people. Some of this appears in the courtly irony with which Chaucer describes the Churchmen and women who rode as pilgrims to Canterbury; much more in the angry poetry in which Langland voiced the grievances of Piers Plowman, on whose underpaid labour the whole structure of luxury and vice depended. John Wyclif went further, sending out poor preachers to read aloud portions of the Scriptures which he had translated to the villagers and preach a Christianity which found no place for well-fed bishops, or lords who flaunted the new Italian fashions in the faces of the poor. Wyclif was condemned for heresy in the end and his followers, known as Lollards, were persecuted out of existence, but not before they had helped to inflame an already very dangerous situation.

The political situation was as threatening as the social. Edward I's policy of marrying the more dangerous feudatories into the royal family had surrounded the King with overmighty cousins to whom rebellion seemed merely a family quarrel, and who were now, thanks to Edward III, permanently organised for war. When the French war petered out with the loss of all the English gains save Calais, Bordeaux and Bayonne, a mass of unemployed soldiers was added to the bands of landless men and fugitive villeins who already haunted the forest fringes and made every highway unsafe, placing a mass of inflammable material at the disposal of an idle and selfish baronage, while the accession of the ten-year-old Richard II in 1377 added all the perils of a long minority and a failure of power at the centre.

The social explosion came first, in 1381, touched off by high taxation, another result of the disastrous war. Inflammatory sermons and rhymes by a preaching friar named John Ball had already set the peasantry wondering "When Adam delved and Eve span, Who was then the gentleman?", and dreaming of a world without tithe or taxation, rich or poor, in which "The King's Son of Heaven shall pay for all", when an old soldier, Wat Tyler, turned out the men of Kent to protest against an inequitable Poll Tax. Essex followed suit, and the discontented workers of London opened the city gates to the rebels. Indecision and disunity among the authorities let what had started as a comparatively orderly protest march degenerate into a murderous rabble which opened the prisons, broke into the Tower, murdered the Treasurer and the Archbishop of Canterbury, and began to loot and burn indiscriminately: and since most of the rest of England was in an uproar, there were no reserves the government could call on.

Young Richard himself saved the situation in London at a moment when a misunderstanding had led to the killing of Wat Tyler by the Mayor and a general massacre seemed imminent. Riding over to the peasant army, he made himself their leader, and led them out of the city walls. With that triumph authority recovered its nerve and the rebellion quickly died away. The mildness of the government's revenge was in itself a confession that the peasant grievances had been well founded: only 200 of the ringleaders, including John Ball, were hanged. But the official classes continued the useless struggle against economic facts, pegging wages back to the 1347 level and re-enforcing villeinage. Since landlords themselves were prepared to bribe their neighbours' villeins away with wages six times the official rate, it was not, in fact, very long before villeinage disappeared, though the peasants paid for their freedom with the loss of their holdings and became landless labourers; and widespread discontent continued throughout Richard's reign. In the long run the sufferings of the poor were only alleviated by the new prosperity which came to the country with the extension of sheep-farming as a result of the Black Death. Exports of English cloth had risen from 7,000 pieces a year to 50,000 by 1395. Food prices fell and wages gradually rose. But as late as 1390 there was a rhyme reminiscent of John Ball's still circulating which ran:

"The axe was sharp and the stokke was hard
In ye XIII yere of King Richarde."

1381 was Richard's last success in dealing with his multifold problems. He had inherited the flaming temper of the Angevins, but not their ability. He hankered after an autocracy, but was too arrogant, petulant, idle, and luxurious to make it effective. The barons, shut out from power by a civilised, dilettante circle of royal relations and favourites who patronised the arts and dabbled amateurishly in government, formed a band of 'Lords

Appellant' even more dangerous than Edward II's 'Ordainers'. For they included an uncle and cousin of the King; their estates and private armies were larger; and behind them they had a truculent, self-confident Parliament exasperated by Richard's dilatory misgovernment and, less reasonably, by a peace with France which, it was felt, dishonoured the memory of his father, the Black Prince.

A brief flurry of civil war in 1387 left the Appellants in power and Richard's friends dead or exiled. Two years later he recovered power, executed or banished his more dangerous opponents, and for ten years ruled as a tyrant, levying high taxes without Parliamentary consent, moving everywhere with an armed guard, and substituting his declared will for the law of England. Finally the sequestration of all the vast estates of his cousin, Henry Bolingbroke, Duke of Lancaster, united the propertied classes solidly against him; he was imprisoned in the Tower and induced to send Parliament a formal abdication of the throne. The rightful heir was undoubtedly Roger Mortimer, grandson of Lionel of Clarence, Edward III's second son. But Mortimer was an infant and Henry was on the spot, all-powerful. He easily induced Parliament to recognise him as King Henry IV, and Richard was sent off to Pontefract to die a few months later, almost certainly murdered.

Now that the Plantagenets had turned upon each other, civil war was inevitable. Always conscious of his shaky title, Henry IV dared not ask Parliament for the large sums needed to restore order, nor could he deal firmly and high-handedly with nobles whose rebellion had put him on the throne and might so easily put him off it again. Even so, there were three great conspiracies in his reign, the first of which brought together the Mortimers and Percies and a last flicker of Welsh nationalism under Owen Glendower and was only defeated by the narrowest of margins at Shrewsbury, the heaviest battle fought on English soil since Hastings. In 1413 Henry died, ill, exhausted, prematurely old, having enjoyed little comfort on his usurped throne There had been ceaseless treachery, executions without trial, and two pitched battles between armies of Englishmen. In effect, the Wars of the Roses had already begun.

Yet the next King, Henry V, had all the qualities which might have averted them. Remorselessly efficient, severely pious in reaction against a wild youth spent in the London taverns, a first-class soldier and administrator, he had every quality of leadership. But, dogged like all the Lancastrians by the consciousness of usurpation and murder, he preferred to divert abroad the dangerous power and energy of the nobles which he should have broken. At Agincourt in 1415 he defeated five times his own numbers, largely by intelligent handling of his archers, and not only saved his starving army from apparently inevitable doom, but so smashed the French field forces that the conquest of France became thereafter a mere matter of systematic annexation. Instead of the old looting and ransom-hunting there was a businesslike occupation, in which each province was immediately expected to pay its own way; and had Henry lived even into middle age there was little to prevent him from subduing the whole of France. But in 1422 he died, worn out by too iron a self-discipline, at a moment when, married to the French King's daughter and formally recognised as his heir, he had the prize within his grasp.

England was to pay a heavy price for this legendary glory. Henry VI, heir to both England and France, was a nine-month-old baby who was to grow into a man of less than normal capacity. The government of a nation almost ruined by war taxation was thus at the mercy of cliques of nobles more powerful and dangerous than ever, thanks to their war service. Moreover, from 1428 onwards a French national revival inspired by Joan of Arc absorbed all the energies of the King's more competent uncle, John, Duke of Bedford. Government at home was carried on by the other uncle, Humphrey of Gloucester, and a camarilla containing most of the future Yorkists, including Richard of York himself who had, through his Mortimer mother, the best hereditary claim to the throne. In a rival gang, periodically strong enough to seize temporary power, were the future Lancastrians: the Beauforts, legitimised cousins of the King, debarred by letters patent from the throne but nursing ambitions none the less, and John de la Pole, Duke of Suffolk, who alone of them all showed a touch of greatness and patriotism. To this last group was added, in 1444, Henry's Queen, Margaret of Anjou, whose enemies called her the she-wolf, and who had all the energy, ferocity, and ambition which her husband lacked.

England's political history from 1423 to 1455 was thus a dreary record of treachery, incompetence, and failure. Though they captured and burnt Joan of Arc in 1431, the English could not hold France. By 1453 only Calais was left and the Hundred Years' War was over. Bedford had died, worn out, in 1435. Gloucester and Suffolk had been murdered, and the King had gone mad. York made himself Regent, but in 1454 the King recovered his wits and turned again to the Beauforts. To save his neck York had to fight, and with the battle of St. Albans in 1455 the Wars of the Roses officially began.

The social effects of this collapse of power at the centre were naturally disastrous. Noblemen kept armies of retainers and levied private war on their neighbours. Cornish pirates, protected by magistrates who were themselves shareholders in their ventures, made the Channel unsafe for shipping. Highways were infested by robbers, and there was a fresh outbreak of land-grabbing by powerful men who terrorised the law courts with bands of armed retainers whom they brought to "maintain their cause". It is true that in spite of all this England was getting steadily richer. There were new goldsmiths' shops in Cheapside, and each year more ships left the London wharves with wool and unfinished cloth for the Flemish factories. Local war did not prevent many sheep farmers from making fortunes, and everywhere new, unfortified manor houses showed the growing prosperity of a lesser gentry remote from the feuds of the Court. Churches, abandoned unfinished at the Black Death, were completed with splendid new perpendicular chancels or west windows, and there was more glorious building to reflect this rising national prosperity in Oxford and Cambridge, and in the King's great new foundation at Eton. Only political stability was lacking.

The futile struggle in which the old nobility and the House of Plantagenet eventually destroyed themselves lasted off and on for thirty years. The wretched Henry VI became a sort of prize of war, used by York or Neville as the figurehead of a 'Protectorate', or briefly and precariously set on the throne again by the fierce energy of his wife. In 1461 he was deposed and shut in the Tower, and the young heir of the House of York had himself crowned as Edward IV, but he was out again eight years later, dirty, ill-kept and feeble-witted, when the over-mighty Richard Neville, Earl of Warwick, 'the King Maker', changed sides unexpectedly, and it was not until the spring of 1471 that the Lancastrian cause finally collapsed, when Warwick was defeated at Barnet and Margaret at Tewkesbury. Both Warwick and Edward, the Lancastrian Prices of Wales, were killed, and soon after Henry VI himself disappeared, almost certainly murdered by Edward IV's brother, Richard, Duke of Gloucester.

Edward was still only thirty, a brilliant soldier and a competent administrator, whose popularity in the City of London gave him plenty of wealthy backing. There was, moreover, no feudal combination strong enough to challenge him. The slaughter of nobles which followed every battle had crippled all the great families : four Beauforts were killed or executed between 1455 and 1471, leaving only an heiress, the Lady Margaret, and her son, Henry Tudor, Earl of Richmond, to carry on that tenuous Lancastrian claim to the throne; and of Warwick's branch of the Nevilles there were only two daughters, each married to one of Edward's brothers. But all these advantages Edward threw away in luxury, idleness, and self-indulgence, and when he died in 1483 he left his two young sons at the mercy of his unscrupulous brother, Gloucester, who promptly had himself crowned as Richard III.

Richard had already begun the self-destruction of the House of York by persuading Edward to have their other brother, Clarence, murdered in the Tower, and within two years he completed it. In spite of many attempts to white-wash him, there can be no reasonable doubt that he murdered his two nephews, the 'little princes'; and in a fresh crop of treasons Lords Rivers, Grey, and Hastings and the Duke of Buckingham lost their heads. Inevitably treachery begat fresh treachery. The good will which Richard might have enjoyed as the strong man saving the country from the anarchy of a long minority quickly evaporated, and he had made too many men afraid of him. When Henry Tudor landed in his native Wales in 1485 he could command little active Lancastrian support, and he faced Richard for the decisive battle at Bosworth with only 5,000 men. But his promise to marry Elizabeth, Edward IV's daughter, held out some hope of ending the long feud for good : and men who feared to take up arms against Richard still would not fight for him. Of the 10,000 he brought to Bosworth half hung back from the fight, and one whole wing under Lord Stanley changed sides by previous arrangement as soon as it started. Fighting magnificently himself, Richard was at last cut down, still furiously shouting 'Treason'; and with him the Plantagenets came to an end.

CHAPTER VII

The Building of Modern England
The Early Tudors
1485 – 1558

THE chance of reasserting the authority of the Crown and the rule of law which was missed by Edward IV after Barnet was eagerly seized by Henry VII after Bosworth. Battles, executions, and forfeitures of land had seriously weakened the feudal magnates and greatly enriched the Crown. He had behind him, more powerful because more wealthy than ever before, the massive support of merchants and small gentry who longed to see highways and sea routes properly policed, the common law properly enforced, and the major disorders of civil war finally suppressed. Moreover, though he was careful to be crowned first in his own right as a Lancastrian, he took the sting out of any possible Yorkist claim by duly marrying Elizabeth, the White Rose of York.

With all these factors in his favour Henry at once attacked what were, in fact, only the old abuses of local power which had plagued Saxon, Norman, and Plantagenet kings alike; and his methods, too, were essentially the old ones. At the core of his problem were the twin evils of Livery and Maintenance : the bands of indentured servants, far beyond their household needs, which great men kept as the nucleus of a private army; and the use of such men to terrorise the law courts. To reassert the authority of the ordinary courts Henry placed behind them his Council, also by immemorial tradition a court of law. A committee of King's Councillors sitting in the Star Chamber was too formidable a body to be terrorised, and all cases where there was danger of the exploitation of the poor and weak by the powerful and wealthy were hauled up to be dealt with there, mostly by heavy fines which had the additional advantage that they increased the royal revenue.

Clear-headed and hardworking, though unspectacular, Henry himself presided with businesslike efficiency over his own Council, and he made it his principal instrument in every reform. Like most of his predecessors, he preferred to staff it with promoted men dependent on himself, or with Churchmen who could not build up a dangerous hereditary wealth and influence. He used the same sort of man on the Councils of the North and of Wales which he set up at York and Ludlow to deal with the especially over-mighty Marcher Lords and bring his justice within the reach of poor men who could not afford the journey to a distant court at Westminster. It was in this ubiquitous and closely supervised activity of his Council and perhaps even more in the weekly personal check of his own account books that the secret of Henry's success lay.

It was the Angevin trick to use law, rather than blind force, for the enforcement of royal authority. It was also in accordance with Angevin precedent to use Parliament to mobilise the support of those classes most directly interested in the preservation of law and order. Parliament passed the final statutes forbidding Livery and Maintenance, and an Act of 1487 confirmed the establishment of the Court of Star Chamber; and from the classes represented in Parliament—the lesser gentry, the merchants, and the lawyers—Henry drew the money which made him the richest, and so ultimately the most powerful King England had ever had, partly in Parliamentary subsidies, partly from forced loans or benevolences levied on the rich, which were illegal but tolerated, at first at any rate, as the price of good government. Money would buy the cannon to batter the walls of feudal castles and a mercenary army more dependable in a crisis than the feudally controlled forces which had deserted Richard III at Bosworth. There were only two major attempts to restart the civil wars; one by Lambert Simnel, who pretended to be Clarence's son, the Earl of Warwick, and one by Perkin

Warbeck, who posed as the younger of the princes murdered in the Tower; and both were easily defeated. In 1492, by the Treaty of Etaples, Henry even made foreign war pay, when generous Parliamentary grants enabled him to send an army to Brittany and the French King paid him handsomely to bring it home again.

An intelligent commercial policy completed this collaboration with merchant interests. A great trading agreement with Burgundy—the Magnus Intercursus of 1496—exploited the dominating position built up in the Flemish market for exports of English unfinished cloth, while at the same time the export of raw wool was heavily taxed to encourage the home weaving industry. Navigation laws, insisting that more of London's trade should be carried in English ships, started a great expansion of the merchant navy; and there was a steady whittling away of the privileges and monopolies built up by the Italians and the powerful North German Hanseatic League in the London market. It was great good fortune that shipbuilding and naval activity generally should have just this fillip when the discovery of America and the rounding of the Cape of Good Hope were opening up new power and prosperity for the nations with ocean-going fleets; and the voyage of the Venetian Cabot brothers to Newfoundland under Henry's patronage set the seal on this promise for the future.

Though all this seemed to be ushering in a new age, what Henry VII had really achieved by the time of his death in 1509 was the completion of the tasks at which his predecessors had worked for centuries. It was his son's accession which struck contemporaries as the rising of a sun on a new, Renaissance world; and his own last years were something of an anti-climax. All those who had brought out the best of his kindly tolerance and loyalty were dead : his wife, and the friends who had shared his exile and served so faithfully on his Council. Careful efficiency had degenerated into avarice. His ministers, Empson and Dudley, were encouraged to abuses of power to bring more fines into the Exchequer. He who, in a bloodthirsty age, had made it his boast that even traitors taken in arms were given a second chance, became mean and suspicious and ended his days in an atmosphere of grumbling discontent which obscured the tremendous service he had done the country.

Of Henry's four children, Margaret had been married to the Stuart King of Scotland, James IV, and Mary to Louis XII of France, while Arthur, the Prince of Wales, had died soon after his marriage to Katherine of Aragon, daughter of Ferdinand and Isabella of Spain. The throne therefore went to the younger son, Henry, who had all the spectacular qualities his father lacked. He was tall and good-looking, intelligent, and beautifully educated, so that he could exchange learned little Latin notes with Erasmus at the dinner table and compose music some of which is played to this day. In his spoilt middle age he was to show himself arrogant, treacherous, and cruel, but none of this showed in the golden-hearted cheerful boy of the prosperous early days when every youthful appetite could easily be gratified: "the best-dressed sovereign in the world", who left cares of state to that able son of an Ipswich butcher who became Cardinal Wolsey, and was, so one of the foreign ambassadors wrote, interested only in "girls and hunting".

With the accession of Henry VIII the Wars of the Roses receded into history and England began to reap the harvest of her 15th-century renaissance. From a mass of newly founded grammar schools and an Oxford enriched by the splendid bequest of Duke Humphrey's library and no longer catering exclusively for future clerics, there had emerged the J.P.s and Councillors and Members of Parliament on whom Henry VII had rested his power. Eton and Winchester had been founded specifically to meet the needs of the more aristocratic of these young men, and in the great London Inns of Court they completed their education with a sound grounding in English law. In 1477 Caxton brought back from Germany the printing press which supplied this new world with the books it needed, and England was producing scholars who could match all that was best in the European revival of learning: Grocyn and Linacre, Dean Colet of St. Paul's, and Sir Thomas

More, the friend of Erasmus who was to become Henry VIII's Chancellor. From the new, Italianate manor houses the younger sons came up to London to seek a fortune at Court, at the Bar, or in the counting house, and wealth flowed back into the countryside as the Merchant Adventurers opened up new markets and the richer city men retired to build their country houses and merge in turn with the gentry. Out of this fabric the so-called new Tudor aristocracy was made. New families, Cecils and Russells, Knollys and Dudleys, and a hundred more, had in fact been growing in numbers, power, and wealth for centuries. They were Tudor only in that they had now ousted the old feudal nobility from the dominating position in government and country and were making their ramifying influence decisive in every department of the national life.

The new reign opened light-heartedly. Empson and Dudley were executed. The King set cheerfully about squandering his father's hoarded wealth, while Wolsey, Cardinal, Archbishop of York, Papal Legate, and Chancellor maintained, it was said, a splendour greater than the King's. The attempt to win another Agincourt in 1513 failed because the French at the Battle of the Spurs refused to stay and fight, though there was grim enough fighting that same year at Flodden, when James IV came over the border to relieve pressure on Scotland's oldest ally and suffered a defeat at the hands of the Earl of Surrey from which it took Scotland a generation to recover. The climax of this period came, perhaps, with the Field of the Cloth of Gold in 1519, when Henry and Wolsey met Francis I of France in tents of silk with gilded cords, and their courtiers invested fortunes in clothes and jewels. Then the note began to change. Cherishing a futile dream of recovering the Angevin empire in France, Henry went to war again, with the Emperor, Charles V, as his ally, ran heavily into debt, and gained nothing, even when Francis was captured by the Imperialists at Pavia in 1525, since the Emperor made the best terms he could without reference to the extravagant English claims. High taxation caused trouble with Parliament and provoked in the end widespread riots; and a further note of gloom was added by the collapse of Henry's private life.

At his accession Henry had married his brother's widow, Katherine, obtaining for the purpose a Papal dispensation, and though she was years older than he was, they had been very happy. Their daughter, Mary, was, however, their only child, and without a son Henry began to feel the Tudor succession insecure. Quite genuinely he seems to have believed that Katherine's miscarriages were God's judgement on a sinful marriage, and he demanded that Wolsey should get the Pope to pronounce the earlier dispensation invalid and so set him free. Unfortunately at that moment Rome was in the hands of Charles V's troops and the Pope dared do nothing to offend him; and Charles was Katherine's nephew.

Out of this deadlock grew the English Reformation. Henry had earned from the Pope the title of Defender of the Faith by writing against Luther, and he had no intention of changing England's religion. Nor had there been any widespread English response to Luther's teaching. Occasional burnings showed that in London and in pockets in the West Country Lollardy still lingered on, and there were popular grievances against the Roman Church : the immunity of the clergy from the King's justice, the vast expense of Papal taxation, the ostentatiously luxurious lives of many of the higher clergy, and the ignorance and vice common among ordinary priests and monks. But these were all remediable. Leaders of Church opinion in England had themselves been clamouring for reform, and there was nothing heretical in demanding, as Henry II had long since, an overhaul of the financial and legal relations between Church and State.

It soon became obvious, however, that the Pope was merely dragging out the divorce negotiations in the hope that he could somehow avoid quarrelling either with Henry or the Emperor; and Wolsey, as a Cardinal of the Church, was clearly a useless instrument for an attack on Rome. So Henry took charge himself. Knowing that he ran a bigger risk of alienating public opinion than any king had dared to take since the disaster of Becket, he

called Parliament together in 1529 and year by year
bullied an often reluctant House of Commons into shear-
ing away the Pope's English revenues—First Fruits and
Tenths, Annates and Peter's Pence. Undoubtedly Henry
expected the Pope to give way under this pressure, but
gradually he found the new sources of power and wealth
which were opening out before him irresistible; and in
1534 he completed the destruction of Papal power in
England by the Act of Supremacy, which declared the
King, 'under God', Supreme Head of the English Church,
and so solved out of hand all the problems which had
vexed his predecessors. The clergy became subject to his
criminal jurisdiction and paid their taxes to him; and he
appointed his own bishops.

Wolsey meanwhile had died in disgrace, and Thomas
Cranmer, whom Henry made Archbishop of Canterbury, had obtained sufficient support among Churchmen
and from universities abroad to feel justified in pronouncing the King's divorce without further reference to Rome.
In great haste in 1533 Henry married Anne Boleyn, who
was already his mistress, but the new marriage was even
less successful than the old. She, too, could produce only
one daughter, Elizabeth, and Henry had her beheaded on
a trumped-up charge of treason in 1536. His third wife,
Jane Seymour, did indeed give him a son, Edward, born
in 1537, but died in doing so; and though he was to marry
again three times, he had no more children. He had, however, achieved his primary object in breaking from Rome,
and had furthermore carried the bulk of influential English opinion with him in doing so. Only in 1535 were there
serious signs of opposition, when Sir Thomas More,
Bishop Fisher of Rochester, and some Carthusian monks
paid with their lives for refusing to take the oath of
Supremacy.

Sheer avarice probably drove Henry on to his next step
—the dissolution of the monasteries, which between them
owned something like a third of the cultivated land in
England, and the sequestration of their wealth. The propaganda justification for this was provided by a systematic visitation under an able lawyer named Thomas Crom-

well, who was invested for the purpose with the Royal Supremacy as 'Vicar General'; and all the evidence he produced of depravity and corruption among monks and nuns, extracted as it was by threats and bribes, is entirely worthless. But there had been plenty of evidence for centuries of monastic laxness and worldliness, of religious duties unperformed, of luxury and vice which went almost unpunished, of shortage of numbers, inefficient administration, and decaying buildings and property. These could easily be worked up into a horrifying picture of wild immorality which salved the consciences of those who bought monastery lands to round off an estate or accepted them as rewards for loyal service. So in 1536 the lesser monasteries, and in 1539 all the remainder, were abolished by Act of Parliament. Thrown on the world, many of the monks went to swell the army of 'sturdy vagabonds' —the wandering, able-bodied unemployed who were a perpetual Tudor problem. The buildings, some of the loveliest of mediaeval architecture, were adapted as mansions or stripped of all that was valuable and left as quarries for local builders and road-makers.

These sweeping changes ushered in one of the most miserable periods of English history. Widespread discontent culminated in 1536 in a rising of the whole north of England known as the Pilgrimage of Grace, which was really a conservative protest against all that the Tudor monarchy stood for, though the pretext was provided by the monasteries which in those bleak uplands still fulfilled vital social as well as religious functions. It gathered at its height 40,000 fighting men at York; armed monks to strike a blow for the dying authority of Rome; peasants exasperated by enclosures for sheep-farming; townsmen whose ancient guild liberties were being undermined by a new capitalism; and Percies, Darcies, and Dacres out to save a remnant of their border independence from the encroaching Council at York. This diversity made it easy for Henry to disperse the rebel army and exact a fearful revenge. But he had clearly shaken English society to its foundations, and when, brutal, suspicious, and tyrannical, he at last died in 1547 he knew that he had released forces which he could not control. There was another peasant rising in the west in 1549 very similar to the Pilgrimage, and an upheaval in Norfolk under one, Robert Kett, who preached a primitive Christian communism reminiscent of John Ball. Meanwhile, the teaching of continental Protestantism was spreading fast among the educated classes in spite of the Six Articles of 1540 in which Henry sought to reassert the basic doctrines of the Roman faith.

During the minority of Edward VI, from 1547 to 1553, and the five-year reign of his sister, Mary, the situation got steadily worse. Power passed into the hands of a predatory land-owning class whom the first of Edward's regents, Edward Seymour, Duke of Somerset, was too mild to control, and who were openly encouraged and abetted by John Dudley, Duke of Northumberland, who ousted Somerset in 1549 and subsequently beheaded him. Enthusiastically supported by the precociously intelligent King, government policy swung violently to the Protestant extreme, producing in the first English Prayer Book of 1549 a lovely piece of prose inspired by Cranmer's gentleness and moderation, which was none the less offensive to conservative folk in remote counties who knew little of the 'new thought'. Under cover of this, Chantries—the endowments for the saying of masses for dead men's souls —were abolished, and all guilds outside London; and their wealth, much of it appropriated to hospitals and schools, was parcelled out among the governing class. Commissioners went round rousing fierce opposition in the villages by smashing the images and pictures in their churches and pillaging their shrines; and in 1552 Northumberland produced an even more extremist Prayer Book which represented the views of only a small, educated minority. Meanwhile the coinage, already debased by Henry VIII, was further devalued, and this, coming on top of a general rise in European prices which was to continue for the rest of the century, created a major economic crisis. The government was all but bankrupt. Landlords, struggling to maintain themselves in a world of rising prices, did all they could to pass the burden on to their tenants by ruthless enclosure, by reviving old customary dues unlevied for centuries, upsetting copyhold leases, rack-renting, and every kind of extortion; and the real value of wages went steadily down.

By 1558 these various causes, religious, economic, and political, had brought England almost to ruin and to the verge of civil war. The poor, with their wages cut to starvation levels, had been deprived of the hospitals and schools, almshouses and infirmaries with which monasteries and guilds and chantry endownments had alleviated their sufferings, and there was probably more real misery throughout the country than at any time since the Black Death. Christ, the reforming Bishop Ridley said in a famous sermon, lay in the streets of London, "hungry, naked and cold", and the nation was in danger of being plunged back into anarchy by the extremist advocates of two religions which had already come to blows in Germany and soon would in France and Holland.

Northumberland had forced himself into power as the strong man who had ruthlessly suppressed Kett's rebellion, and he was never popular, especially after his execution of Somerset, whose sympathy for the sufferings of the poor, though ineffectual, was widely known. His future therefore depended absolutely on the favour of the cold, hard, intellectual young King, and his Prayer Book of 1552 had been a gamble to obtain it. But the gamble went wrong. Edward rapidly sickened and died of consumption, and the next heir, by Act of Parliament and Henry VIII's will, was Mary, daughter of the divorced Katherine, a devoted, passionate, and embittered Catholic. Northumberland made a desperate effort to save himself by putting his Protestant daughter-in-law, Henry VIII's niece, Lady Jane Grey, on the throne, but public opinion, intensely conservative and bewildered by the violent changes of the last seven years, turned decisively against him. Mary had all the Tudor courage and a will of her own, and when she raised her standard a wave of popularity swept her into power and Northumberland and Queen Jane into the Tower and ultimately to the block.

But Mary in turn went too far and too fast in the other direction. She had the inarticulate masses behind her, but was opposed by a majority of the wealthy and influential, some convinced Protestants, and all fearful that they might have to disgorge their Church lands. She fairly easily induced Parliament to restore the situation as it had existed at Henry VIII's death. But by marrying Philip II of Spain, and by bringing her cousin, Cardinal Pole, from Rome to restore Papal authority she roused passionate opposition. The men of Kent rose under Sir Thomas Wyatt to the cry of 'No Spanish Match', and Londoners broke up her masses. In the thickly populated south-east, Protestantism had begun to spread among the ordinary people, and when Mary was driven to persecute she found she had to burn not only Crammer and the bishops who had led reforming thought, Latimer, Ridley, and Hooper, but a mass of poor, obscure folk whose martyrdom finally rooted Protestantism in the minds of the uneducated. By the time she died she knew that she had failed. Her husband had deserted her. The baby she longed for and believed to be on the way was never born. Her religion was hated and resisted, and she was to go down to history as Bloody Mary. Her Spanish marriage had involved England again in the Spanish war with France, and fate's final blow had been the loss of Calais, England's last proudly held possession in France. She died a bitter, disappointed woman, leaving her throne to the redheaded daughter of Anne Boleyn, Elizabeth, who would almost certainly undo what little she had achieved.

THE TUDORS AND STUARTS

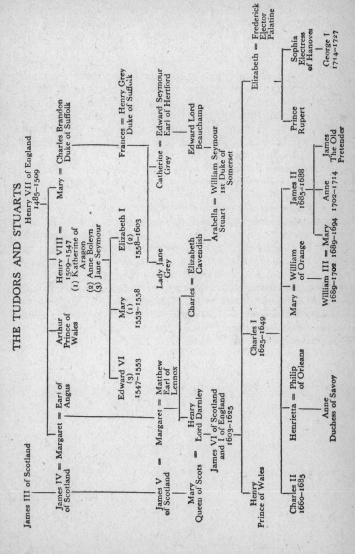

CHAPTER VIII

The Birth Pangs
of Representative Government
1558 – 1628

THANKS to the efficiency of Henry VII, Elizabeth was not faced, as most of her contemporary rulers in Europe perpetually were, by the threat of feudal rebellion or civil war. But in all other respects her situation seemed unenviable. In the eyes of Catholic Europe and of her own Catholic subjects she was the illegitimate usurper of a throne which rightly belonged to Mary Stuart, granddaughter of James IV of Scotland and of Margaret Tudor, Queen of Scots, and married to the Dauphin of France. There was imminent danger of class war and religious war, and a looming threat of invasion from without by one of the great Catholic powers. Trade was bad and there was widespread agrarian discontent. Mary's five disastrous years had confirmed the general belief that no woman could govern England; and the most men hoped for was that the new Queen would find a strong, capable husband to do the job for her.

Elizabeth, however, was an exceptionally talented and intelligent young woman, entirely self-confident, with much of her father's temper and his trick of popularity, but without his streak of vindictive cruelty. Above all she had a tremendous sense of her responsibility to God for the good government of her subjects. From the moment of her first ride through London she caught the English imagination and began to be a legend. Autocratic and eccentric, with the sharpest tongue in the kingdom, she turned her femininity into an asset, inspiring in all classes a loyalty and devotion which no king could have won, and uniting the nation as it had never been united before.

In consequence, most of the major problems were solved with surprising speed and ease. In religion Elizabeth would probably have preferred to go back to the final position of Henry VIII, but Mary's burnings had roused too much hostility. On the other hand the majority of her subjects were still Catholic in outlook and preferred the old worship. As 'Supreme Governor of the Church' she aimed at avoiding both extremes; and her Prayer Book and Thirty-nine Articles of Religion sought to avoid offending the great body of moderate opinion rather than to satisfy any particular group. There was as little doctrinal definition as possible. Phrases in the Communion Service implied both acceptance and rejection of the Real Presence, and the form of the English worship closely conformed to the old Romish pattern. Though all but one of Mary's bishops resigned, enough men were found to staff the new venture, and Elizabeth left it to time and the mild pressure of fines for non-attendance at Church to reconcile the majority of her subjects.

At the same time she went straight to the root of her economic problems. The worst cause of trade dislocation was removed by the issue of a new silver coinage in place of the old debased currency. By 1561 an elaborate system of tariffs and bounties protected new industries and stimulated the exploitation of fresh sources of tin, copper, and zinc. Some, though not yet adequate, steps had been taken to save the surviving oak forests for ship-building. The government found itself again able to borrow money in the City at reasonable rates, and a rudimentary form of welfare state was striving to replace the monasteries and guilds in protecting the poor from exploitation. The J.P.s in each county were required to fix minimum wages for industry, agriculture, and domestic service and to keep the price of bread at a level which enabled the poor to subsist; and the Statute of Apprentices of 1563 did something to ensure proper training, payment, and care for all workmen. The poor were thus saved from the worst effects of a world-wide inflation which no English government could halt, though the struggles of a land-owning gentry to cope with rising prices on largely fixed rent-rolls would still cause acute trouble for the next hundred years. The government could not halt the enclosure and drainage of waste land, which were after all essential for an improving agriculture and an expanding population, but only slow it down so that not too many smallholders were squeezed out into what would today be called redundancy. Thus there was still much unemployment, and almost the last Act of the reign was the amended Poor Law of 1601 making parish overseers responsible under the Justices for finding work for the able-bodied unemployed and providing workhouses for the old and the unemployable.

Time was to prove all these measures just adequate. In spite of a hard core of Catholics and the noisy, dissatisfied Protestant extremists—the Puritans—the Church of England by 1588 commanded the loyalty of a vast majority of Englishmen. Oxford and Cambridge were beginning to meet the need for a trained clergy and a new generation had grown up which knew no other form of worship. Prosperity crept back as the cloth trade re-established itself, and there was a steady flow of new capital into ventures such as the Muscovy and Levant Companies, culminating in the grant of a Royal Charter to the greatest of them all, the East India Company, in 1600. Elizabeth's prime political need—and her most brilliant achievement —was thus to gain this time and confront the inevitable foreign crisis with a united and prosperous nation behind her. It was at first a desperate business, with an imminent threat of French invasion, and even the possibility that France and Spain might heal their long feud by combining in a Catholic crusade against England. Mary Stuart, titular Queen of Scots almost since her birth in 1542, had been brought up a Frenchwoman and until the death of her husband in 1560 was also Queen Consort of France. Elizabeth therefore clung to the traditional Spanish alliance, brilliantly deluding Philip II for years that at any moment she might follow her sister's example and marry him, and so bring both herself and England back into the Catholic fold. At the same time some judicious help in money and ships enabled the new reforming party under John Knox in Scotland to expel the French Regent, so slightly reducing the threat from that quarter.

Gradually this policy of playing for time began to pay dividends. Religious civil war broke out in France. The Netherlands rose in revolt against Spain; and in Scotland the widowed Mary Stuart's five-year struggle to save the country for herself and for Catholicism ended in final defeat at Langside in 1568. Mary fled across the border to become Elizabeth's guest and prisoner for nineteen years. The Franco-Scottish threat thus ceased to exist, while Spain had too much on her hands and was too anxious to keep the Channel open to her fleets to risk embroiling herself with England, especially when victory could only mean putting the French Mary Stuart on the English throne.

Until 1586 Elizabeth was able to exploit this situation, sending just enough help to French, Dutch, and Scottish Protestants to enable them to survive, while her seamen, Drake, Hawkins, the Gilberts and the rest, harried Spanish Plate fleets and colonies, secure in the knowledge that the last thing Philip II wanted was open war with England. In 1581 the Spanish Ambassador even had to attend the knighting of Drake on the quarter-deck of the *Golden Hind* when everybody knew that he had brought back from his voyage round the world a million pound's worth of Spanish loot. Philip could only revenge himself by half-hearted support for Catholic plots on behalf of Mary : Ridolfi's in 1571, Throckmorton's in 1583, and Babington's in 1586, all of which were foiled by the tireless Secretary of State, Sir Francis Walsingham, and which were a small price to pay for the gold and the vast seafaring experience brought back from the Indies by Drake and his friends.

This was not, however, a game which could be played for ever. It became necessary to send the Queen's favourite, Leicester, with 10,000 men to save the Dutch from extinction, and the fiction of peace could no longer be maintained. Moreover, Mary's intercepted letters showed that, exasperated by her long captivity, she had made Philip her heir in England and Scotland and had also formally approved Babington's conspiracy, so that Philip could build his Armada without feeling that he was merely feathering a French nest and there was no longer any reason to keep Mary alive. As early as 1569 a rising of the northern earls on Mary's behalf had shown that there was little general enthusiasm left for the Catholic cause, and since then the plots and the legends of the Spanish Inquisition's brutality to captured English seamen had united the whole country in a frenzy of Protestant and patriotic loyalty. So every factor combined to precipitate the crisis. In 1587 Mary was executed for her complicity in Babington's conspiracy, and that summer the Armada would have sailed had not Drake "singed the King of Spain's beard" by burning half the fleet in Cadiz harbour. A year later Elizabeth refused to let him repeat the exploit, and at long last the beacons on every hill told a waiting England that the Armada had been sighted off the Lizard.

Its task was not to destroy the English fleet, but to convoy the Prince of Parma's powerful army across the Channel from Dunkirk; and probably the famous Spanish infantry would have made short work of the 70,000 enthusiastic but untrained militiamen who gathered at Tilbury to hear their Queen tell them that she had come "to live or die amongst you all." Fortunately the seamen managed the job for themselves. Using the running gun-fight tactics worked out by Drake, they herded the Spaniards up the Channel for nearly a week and, as the Admiral, Lord Howard of Effingham wrote, "plucked their feathers little by little." But the Armada was still quite capable of bringing Parma across if he had been ready when it anchored off Calais, and the English were desperately short of gunpowder. It was the next two days' fighting which settled the issue. Fireships drifted in with the tide panicked the Spaniards into cutting their cables, and as they scattered north-eastwards even shorter of powder than the English, they were decisively defeated. When it re-formed the Armada was still, as Drake said, "wondrous strong", but it could not beat its way back into the Channel and it had no stomach for further fighting. Atlantic gales, as it worked its way back to Spain round the north of Scotland

and Ireland, completed its ruin, and out of 130 ships only 53 got home. The English lost only 60 men.

After this great climax things went less well for Elizabeth. She could not find men of the same stature to replace those who had served her so well through the crisis : statesmen like Lord Burleigh and Walsingham, efficient, level-headed and utterly devoted; courtiers like Sir Philip Sidney who could write great poetry as well as show the world how a gentleman should die, or Leicester who was not only attractive, but a useful councillor and a competent army commander; seamen whose names have become household words. Drake and Hawkins were replaced by Essex, volatile, spectacular, and unreliable, who captivated the ageing Queen, but fell in the end into treason and had to be beheaded. The whole burden of politics fell gradually on to Sir Robert Cecil, Burleigh's hunch-backed younger son, who was well trained and devoted, but without imaginative genius. A long-drawn-out war with Irish rebels cost England far more than she could afford. Some of the later expeditions against Spanish fleets and harbours achieved fame, such as Essex's sacking of Cadiz in 1596 and Grenville's last fight in the *Revenge*, but there was no real success. Though in literature and architecture England's great age was only just beginning, and all the greatest work of Shakespeare, Ben Jonson, Inigo Jones, and a host of lesser men was still to come, in all other respects Elizabeth's world was declining. She wrangled with Parliament over religion and trade and her popularity slowly waned. Thus the accession of Mary Stuart's son, James VI of Scotland and I of England, was not really the shocking anti-climax historians have sometimes made out. The Virgin Queen had already become a glamorous legend when James succeeded to all the problems created by the Tudors.

For the Tudor achievement carried with it certain inevitable penalties. They had broken feudalism, completed a religious reformation without civil war, and fought off the most serious external threat England had faced since the Conquest, and had done it without a standing army and without weakening England's fundamental laws and liberties. Perforce they had relied throughout on the massive support of the gentry—the great land-owning nobles, country squires of infinitely varying wealth, lawyers and city merchants—who supplied their councillors and Officers of State, their officials and courtiers, their soldiers and sea-captains, and the unpaid Lords Lieutenant, sheriffs, and magistrates who administered every county and dominated every borough council. In the last analysis all Tudor power rested on the intelligent co-operation of this governing class, which was also the class represented in Parliament. In practice nobody could safely defy Henry VIII; but even he recognised that the ultimate sovereign was the King in Parliament which, as the Commons themselves once put it, was "a single body politic". It had thus been essential to encourage in Parliament a greater sense of its own importance and a closer and more continuous interest in matters of state. Otherwise its support was valueless.

In destroying the baronage, expelling Papal power and despoiling the monasteries, and in the struggle for national survival against Spain, the interests of Crown and Commons had been roughly identical. But when the crisis passed there were bound to arise differences over which a more self-confident and businesslike House of Commons would begin to assert its own point of view. It would demand some say in the spending of the taxes which it voted; and as Puritanism spread, especially among the educated classes, it would inevitably challenge the Royal Supremacy in matters of religion. Elizabeth forbade all discussion of religion in Parliament and punished disobedience with imprisonment, but in the end she had to give way and in 1597 she actually invited the Commons to debate certain specific points of "Ecclesiastical Reformation". And she only staved off a crisis on financial questions by methods which made the problem worse for her successor. In a world of rising prices the Crown, with a fixed income derived mainly from rents, feudal dues, and the customs duties known as Tunnage and Poundage, got steadily poorer. Hating to incur unpopularity by high taxation, Elizabeth concealed the real state of affairs from Parliament, partly by stringent economy, partly by the sale of Crown lands and of Monopolies, which were intended as an early patent system, but which easily degenerated into exploitation of the consumer by unscrupulous courtiers or royal servants. Even so she bequeathed to James a deficit of £400,000 incurred over the Irish war; and she had a major row over Monopolies in 1601, when she had to cancel most of her grants, though she managed her surrender so gracefully as to provoke an outburst of loyal gratitude from the Commons.

James I had not the political skill, the charm, nor the accumulated prestige of Elizabeth. He lacked both dignity and courage. His legs were weak and rickety, his tongue was too large for his mouth, and he wore his clothes quilted and padded for fear of assassination. Even his qualities—his fine academic brain, and his easy familiarity—were handicaps to a king; and he knew little of English history or law. By 1611, when he dissolved his first Parliament, he had failed either to find a new religious settlement which would prevent the growing Puritan party from going into open opposition, or a financial agreement which would have stopped the endless bickerings with the Commons over money; and the English Civil War was the ultimate consequence of his failure.

The turning-point in religion was the Hampton Court Conference of 1604, where the Puritan representatives met the bishops under the chairmanship of the King, who prided himself on his theological skill, to discuss their grievances, which they had already embodied in what was know as the Millenary Petition. These were not actually very serious : requests that the wearing of vestments and surplices be optional and that the use of the sign of the cross in baptism and the ring in marriage be discontinued, and that bishops should accept the advice and assistance of elected synods on the Presbyterian model. But James had already had a trying time with the Scottish Presbyterians and he was bent above all on preserving his Divine Right; that mystical trust held from God of which no man-made ordinance could deprive him. He saw that this and the bishops' claim to apostolic authority must stand or fall together. "No Bishop, no King" was the core of his belief, and when the Puritans talked of the Presbyterian system he lost his temper altogether, vowing to "harry out of the land" all who would not conform to the Thirty-nine Articles. Only 300 clergy lost their livings in consequence, but these "300 silenced brethren" gave the Commons a grievance to harp on for the next twenty years and quite overshadowed the one great achievement of the conference—the undertaking of the Authorised Version of the Bible which was to be the greatest monument of Elizabethan prose.

The financial situation deteriorated even more sharply. Cecil, whom the King made Earl of Salisbury and Treasurer, tried to save the situation by the imposition of extra customs duties by royal authority over and above what Parliament had voted the King for life as Tunnage and Poundage. In Bate's famous case the judges upheld the King, but the Commons were infuriated by the thought of the royal finances slipping out of their control altogether and fought back fiercely. James, too, was extravagant, flinging money about to worthless favourites and courtiers and squandering it on wild, undignified, drunken parties; and in seven years his debts were doubled. Moreover, on top of the Hampton Court decisions he exasperated a majority of his subjects by tolerating Catholics, relaxing their fines and taking them into high favour at Court. He persisted in this even after the Gunpowder Plot of 1605, when a handful of fanatics employed Guy Fawkes to try to destroy the whole governing class at a blow; and this enlightened tolerance destroyed what chance Salisbury still had with the Commons when he tried to negotiate his 'Great Contract' in 1610. The Commons attached so many conditions, religious and financial, to the grant of a larger permanent income to the Crown that James at last dissolved them in disgust and tried for ten years to rule without Parliament altogether.

The record of those ten years made an even worse situation when Parliament met again in 1621. Every unpopular device—Impositions, Forced Loans, Monopolies, and the sale of rank and office—had been used to get the money Parliament would not vote, and every religious prejudice outraged by negotiations for a Spanish wife for the heir to the throne. England had acquiesced in the peace which James had made with Spain in 1604, but rebelled at the thought of intimate alliance. Finally the King's passion for worthless young men had led him to entrust supreme power first to Robert Carr, Earl of Somerset, who crashed in the noisiest scandal of the century in 1615, when his wife was found to have secured her divorce by murdering his best friend; and then to a more pleasant but far more dangerous young man, George Villiers, who was made Duke of Buckingham.

Buckingham was conceited, extremely greedy of office and profit for himself and his family, and with just enough intelligence to fancy himself a statesman. Unfortunately his rise coincided with the outbreak of the Thirty Years' War, one result of which was the expulsion from his dominions of the Protestant Elector Palatine who had married James's popular daughter, Elizabeth. Protestant England clamoured for her restoration by making war on Spain in the grand old Elizabethan manner. James, peace-loving by nature, hoped to achieve the same result by offering Spain English alliance, a Spanish marriage for his son, and large concessions to English Catholics. An English fleet and army were necessary to back both these unrealistic policies; and, since Parliament was reluctant to vote money for Buckingham to squander, the wrangles of 1610 began again.

In practice James's views were ceasing to matter as he lapsed into sloth and premature senility. Control passed to Buckingham and Prince Charles, who was also Buckingham's slavish adorer; and both were wholly capricious. They went off to Madrid together incognito in 1623 to force the Spaniards to give up the Infanta and returned insulted by Spanish delays to plunge England into war against Spain instead. 12,000 "raw poor rascals", hastily conscripted, untrained and unprovisioned, were sent to free the Palatinate and perished of famine and disease on the island of Walcheren. A naval expedition against Cadiz in 1625 suffered similar disaster. In due course Charles, having first married the French Princess Henrietta Maria, quarrelled with France as well, and England was at war with both the great powers of Europe simultaneously. Yet another expedition, this time led by Buckingham in person and intended to relieve the French Protestant rebels besieged in La Rochelle, ended in disaster in 1627, and there would have been a fourth had not a discontented Puritan officer assassinated Buckingham at Portsmouth on the eve of his embarkation in 1628.

This was the background of the complete breakdown of the King's relations with Parliament which occurred between 1621 and 1629. Exasperated by financial scandals which had already caused the disgrace of a Lord Treasurer and a Lord High Admiral for embezzlement and corruption, the Commons revived the disused weapon of impeachment to attack Monopoly holders and even ministers of the Crown. The philosopher, Francis Bacon, was convicted of taking bribes as Lord Chancellor, and they drove from office the ablest Treasurer James ever had, Lord Middlesex. They refused to vote money until their grievances on Impositions, Monopolies, and Religion were remedied; and they protested their right to free debate so forcibly and offensively that James tore the page recording their protest from their Journals.

When James died in 1625 things went no better. Charles I was a very different man, dignified, severely decorous, and intensely reserved. Only the high sense of his own 'kingship' and the fatal devotion to Buckingham were the same. Mistrusting both, Parliament voted Tunnage and Poundage only for a year at a time and finally provoked its own dissolution by impeaching Buckingham. Meanwhile the grievances mounted. Lords as well as Commoners were imprisoned without trial for opposing the government in Parliament. Troops were billeted on householders without payment, and the victims of military indiscipline forced to depend on illegal courts martial for redress. Charles raised the money Parliament would not vote as a Forced Loan and imprisoned or conscripted for foreign service those who would not pay; and though in the end poverty forced him to give way and accept the

Petition of Right which embodied all these accumulated grievances, he had no real intention of carrying out his promises. The outburst of national rejoicing at Buckingham's murder completed his estrangement from his subjects. In 1629 he dissolved his third Parliament and set out to govern by his own authority alone, ignoring the Petition of Right, and so inaugurating what has come to be known as the Eleven Years' Tyranny.

CHAPTER IX

The Crisis of English History
Civil War. Restoration, Revolution
1628–1688

EVENTS from 1629 to 1640 showed how right the Tudors had been to base their whole system on collaboration with Parliament. Thomas Wentworth, later Earl of Strafford, deserted the opposition at Buckingham's death and eagerly seized the opportunity offered by the King of showing what efficient royal government should be. His policy which he and his friend, Laud, Archbishop of Canterbury, called 'Thorough' was that of all enlightened despotisms everywhere : to give all classes government so good and equitable that clamour about grievances and difficulty in raising taxes would disappear. In spite of an unenthusiastic King and the ceaseless intrigues of unscrupulous colleagues, Strafford succeeded reasonably well, especially in those areas where, as Lord President of the Council of the North and Lord Deputy in Ireland, he directly controlled administration. Magistrates were kept sharply to their duties under the Statute of Apprentices and compelled to build the workhouses they had neglected. An efficient fleet at last patrolled home waters every summer to put down piracy. Wages and prices were equitably fixed. Laud, meanwhile, set himself to achieve the uniformity decreed after Hampton Court in the teeth of the growing Puritan opposition.

To finance all this the law against Monopolies had to be evaded by granting them to corporations instead of to individuals, and Ship Money raised in peacetime and in inland counties, which was logical but unprecedented. Yet Strafford might have won through. For it was a peaceful, prosperous time, with a steady surplus of men and capital flowing out to the American colonies and, until 1635, little openly expressed discontent. John Hampden's famous stand against Ship Money heralded disaster by inducing the propertied classes to withhold their taxes. But it was Laud's attempt to bring back into the churches what he called 'the beauty of holiness' which doomed the system of 'Thorough', since it could only be enforced by fines and the pillory and the sawing off of men's ears; and when he and Charles then tried to force the English Prayer Book on the Scots they provoked the so-called Bishops' Wars for which they could not pay. So in the Long Parliament of 1641 Charles found himself faced with a House of Commons solidly united against him.

The common people might have spoken for Strafford, who had tried to protect them from exploitation; but hardly a single educated or politically important Englishman sympathised with his ideal of a strong, centralised, efficient government which would, if necessary, override the law for the good of the people. His enemies, led by John Pym, when they could fasten no crime on him, turned his own argument against him, and for the good of the people voted his destruction by Bill of Attainder. With the London mob howling round Whitehall and no troops to defend his wife and children, Charles gave way and signed the Bill; and 'Black Tom Tyrant' lost his head on Tower Hill before the biggest rejoicing crowd England had even seen. Thereafter Charles, helpless, had to sign away all the machinery by which Stuart government had been made to work. Star Chamber, the Councils of the North and Wales, and Laud's Court of High Commission were abolished. Monopolies, Impositions, Ship Money, and the like were declared illegal, leaving only taxes voted by Parliament. Judges were made immune from royal interference, and Charles had to pledge himself to call Parliament together at least once in every three years.

So far there could be no civil war because there was no royalist party. Only a handful of courtiers and Roman Catholics who depended entirely on the Court stood by the King. But when Pym and his friends attacked the Bishops and proposed Presbyterian reforms, and at the same time sought to deprive Charles of his most ancient prerogative of commanding the militia, lest he use it against themselves, they gave him a party. Plenty of Anglicans would fight for their Church however much they deplored Laud's sharp, persecuting ways; and Edward Hyde, later Earl of Clarendon, brought across to the King's side a band of political conservatives suddenly frightened that Pym was really playing for a Republic. Hardly anybody who fought for Charles in the Civil War approved of Stuart arbitrary taxation and imprisonment, or of the divine right theories which upset the delicate Tudor balance of King in Parliament as sovereign of England. But now Pym was the innovator, and the alternative tyranny of a majority of the House of Commons they found even more intolerable. When Pym divided the House on the Grand Remonstrance, which rolled all his policies, reasonable and unreasonable, together, he could only get a majority of eleven and civil war became inevitable. After an attempt inspired by the Queen, to arrest five of the opposition leaders on the floor of the House—which only a Strafford might have done successfully—Charles withdrew from London and set up his standard at Nottingham in August 1642, while Parliament began to raise troops in London and the Home Counties.

There was little fundamental difference between the two parties which had hitherto been a compact majority against the King. All classes and all kinds of men were found on both sides. Among the Cavaliers those whose loyalty was part of their religion who would support the King right or wrong; among the Roundheads men of genuine principle who were beginning to think along republican lines. Both sides had their self-interested racketeers; monopolists and profiteers from Court patronage on the one, and self-seeking employers who had resented Strafford's protection of their workers and apprentices on the other. On both sides there were men who fought on religious grounds alone. And the rank and file of both armies mostly followed their masters without much conviction either way: squires turned out their grooms, tenants and cottagers, businessmen their appren-

MAP TO ILLUSTRATE THE
CIVIL WAR

District held by the King
– · – · Parliament

SCOTLAND

NORTH
SEA

Dunbar
Glasgow
Bothwell Brig
1679
Drumclog
1679
D'hiliphaugh
Berwick-on-Tweed
Flodden
1513
Redesdale
Newburn
Newcastle-on-Tyne
Hexham
Carlisle
Durham
Scarborough
Ripon
Lancaster
Marston
Moor
York
Hull
Bradford
Preston
Leeds
Pontefract
Bolton
Liverpool
Manchester
Gainsborough
Lincoln
Wincely
Chester
Newark
Nantwich
Nottingham
Derby
Shrewsbury
Lichfield
Leicester
Norwich

IRISH SEA

WALES

Birmingham
Naseby
Huntingdon
Newmarket
Warwick
Cambridge
Ipswich
Worcester
Bedford
Gloucester
Edge Hill
Colchester
Paglan
Oxford
Pembroke
Newbury
Windsor
LONDON
Reading
Hampton Ct.
Chatham
Maidstone
Canterbury
Winchester
Cheriton
Sedgemoor
Bridgewater
1685
Salisbury
Southampton
Langport
Beachy Head
1692
Taunton
Poole
Exeter
Corisbrook
Lostwithiel
Lyme
Regis
Plymouth
Torbay
Nov 5 1688
Fowey

ENGLISH CHANNEL

tices and journeymen. Most men probably tried to avoid getting involved on either side.

The Civil War was thus a very amateurish affair fought out by tiny minorities. The King at the outset had advantages with which he could have won : hard riding squires and grooms from the remote north and west, and a trained cavalry leader in his nephew, Prince Rupert, who had grown up in the thick of European war. But at Edgehill and in the battles of 1643 the royalists bungled their chances and missed capturing London. The King's money, provided largely from the rents and melted-down plate of his supporters, began to give out, while Parliament, controlling London and the thickly populated south-east, drew far more in direct taxes and got the bulk of the customs duties. They also found in Cromwell the one great general of the war, and he trained for them a properly paid professional force which became the New Model Army, and irresistible. Moreover, Pym, before he died of cancer, brought the highly trained Scottish army in on Parliament's side by promising to make England Presbyterian. The issue was really settled at Marston Moor in 1644, when Rupert was defeated by Cromwell and the Scots and lost the whole of the north. At Naseby a year later the New Model destroyed the last effective royal army, and the war petered out.

Almost immediately men began to realise that the war had settled nothing. All but a handful of republicans wanted monarchy to survive, but nobody could see how to bind the King to keep the laws of 1641, which he regarded as a fundamental infringement of his kingship. London, the Scots, and what remained of the old House of Commons demanded Presbyterianism; Royalists and most of the country folk wanted the old Church, Bishops, and Prayer Book; Cromwell's army, which wielded the only real power in England, stood for freedom for all Protestants to worship as they pleased, which they called Independency. Had he accepted some reasonable safeguards and surrendered command of the militia for ten years, the army would have put Charles back on the throne. Had he declared for Presbyterianism Parliament and the Scots were ready to restore him. But he was courageously loyal to the Church of which he was the anointed Head and, less creditably, tried to play off his enemies against each other in the hope of unconditional restoration. By this he brought down a Scottish army to be defeated by Cromwell at Preston, and in so doing doomed himself. Cromwell and the soldiers, suddenly sick of evasions and tricks by "that man of blood, Charles Stuart", and convinced that God was on their side, brought the King to trial in Westminster Hall for treason to the People. There was, of course, no such thing in law, and Charles in the last weeks of his life won more friends and admirers by his courage and dignity than he had ever commanded as King. The groan which went up from the silent crowd round the scaffold before Whitehall on 30th January, 1649, when his head fell was echoed throughout England and throughout the civilised world. Only Cromwell's own soldiers agreed with him that this was a "cruel necessity"; and by that one act he condemned to immediate failure all the causes for which he had fought.

For it was easy in the England of 1649 to find a majority against any of the available solutions to the problems in Church and State, and this made it impossible for Cromwell to do what he always longed to do—to hand back power to some properly constituted representative authority. For, though a majority had disapproved of Charles I's methods, all but a handful thought King, Lords, and Commons the only proper form of English government. They longed to go, not forward to new experiments, but back to the good old days. There were Levellers in the army who preached an early, primitive Communism and advocated universal suffrage, but they knew that if they had their way their ideas would be voted out of existence. The same was true of all the forms of government which Cromwell tried one after the other. The so-called Commonwealth of England, which meant government by the Rump—the surviving fragment of the Long Parliament—was abolished without regret in 1653. A specially selected body who called themselves the Saints and were known to the country as the Barebones Parliament showed themselves quite unpractical and had to be dismissed. The same happened to the two Parliaments elected under a system called the Instrument of Government devised by the senior army officers. Cromwell dared not trust a free vote, which would sweep him and all his works away, and in the end had to face the facts and govern England as Lord Protector by naked military force, putting each district under a Major-General : a system worse hated than any other government in England has ever been.

It remains true, of course, that Cromwell gave England better government than she had ever had, or was to have again for a long time. Committees of businessmen and professional civil servants took over the old haphazard administration of the state departments by courtiers on the make and ran them very well; and the power and influence of England in the world at large rose to unprecedented heights. Having subdued Ireland, brutally but effectively, forced the Scots to accept the situation by his victory of Dunbar in 1650, and finally driven Charles II into permanent exile at Worcester in 1651, he proceeded to break the disapproval of Europe by force. An enormously enlarged fleet commanded by a sailor of genius, Robert Blake, forced successively the Portuguese, the Spaniards, the French and the Dutch to respect England's right to manage her own affairs, and incidentally added Jamaica to the oversea empire and captured Dunkirk as a fortified outpost in Europe. But it was all very expensive. Cromwell's governments spent three times what Charles I had raised in taxation, and this, too, made men long more than ever for the good old days. A standing army of 50,000 men and a battle fleet of 200 ships were luxuries which England did not wish to afford.

Thus Cromwell's death precipitated a restoration of King and Parliament with astonishing speed and ease. There was no other general who could command the loyalty of the whole army; and once the soldiers got fighting among themselves the nation's real wishes could assert themselves. Cromwell's son, Richard, earned the nickname of Tumbledown Dick by the rapidity of his fall, and there was some danger of civil war between rival generals.

But George Monk, army commander in Scotland, timed his march south in the name of a free Parliament exactly right. Even the soldiers, sick of unpopularity and longing for their arrears of pay to set them up in civilian life, would not fight for Monk's rivals, and the rest of England went mad for joy. For everyone knew that a free Parliament meant the return of Charles I's son and with him the old constitution. The remnants of the Long Parliament were readmitted to Westminster on the understanding that they immediately voted their own dissolution; and the new Parliament—the Convention—duly opened negotiations with Charles II.

It was fortunate for England that Charles's adviser in exile was that Clarendon who, as Edward Hyde, had opposed his father in 1641. Valuing Parliament's privileges as highly as he did the royal prerogative, he ensured that the Restoration was a triumph for neither of the parties which had fought the war. They picked up the threads from the last legal act of the Long Parliament in 1642, and so all the unpopular institutions and practices of James I and Charles I were recognised as illegal by Charles II before he even sat on the throne. Not surprisingly Royalists who had sacrificed rents and plate had fought for the King and suffered exile or imprisonment, had forfeited land or been forced to sell it to pay enormous fines, were bitterly disappointed when Charles and Clarendon denied them revenge. Confiscated land, which included all Church endowments, was returned to the original owners without compensation. What men had been forced to sell to pay Parliamentary fines could not be recovered. So the inevitable grievances were almost equally divided between the two parties. An Act of Indemnity and Oblivion brought a curtain down on all crimes committed against the King, except for that of the actual regicides who had signed Charles I's death warrant. The surviving Anglican clergy resumed their livings and the use of the Prayer Book. The army was paid off, and with surprising ease the old machinery in Church and State came quietly into operation again.

The man who stepped ashore at Dover in May of 1660

in the eleventh year of his reign and rode into London amid scenes of the wildest rejoicing along streets lined by the soldiers who had killed his father was not likely to fight many issues of principle out to a finish. Cheerful, cynical, amusing, and extremely lazy, he lacked both his grandfather's prosy conviction of rightness and his father's intolerable sense of anointed kingship. Ten years of poverty-stricken exile had ruined his morals, but left him very worldly-wise, and he had vowed "never to go on his travels again". He was devoted to his family, intensely loyal to his friends, easy-going to his enemies, and, if forced to action, an astute politician. It was Clarendon, old now, ill-tempered, and arrogant, who really ruled for the next eight years. But his statesmanship was really exhausted when he had achieved the peaceful restoration of King and Parliament. He could not push through the wise policy of religious toleration he had formulated, and between 1662 and 1665 the enthusiastic Cavalier Parliament, which replaced the Convention, enacted the persecuting measures unfairly known as the Clarendon Code which went much further than Bancroft or Laud in tightening up the conditions of Uniformity. 2,000 Puritan clergy were ejected from their livings and forbidden to come within five miles of any borough town. All public worship save the Anglican was banned; and non-conformists were barred from all municipal office.

Apart from this, Clarendon's government did little except involve itself in a naval war with Holland, which it could not win, and suffer undeserved unpopularity for being in power during two national disasters: the Great Plague of 1665 and the Fire of London in 1666. The Plague, the last great visitation of its kind, killed 68,000 people in London alone, and the Fire destroyed £10 million worth of commercial property. With trade at a standstill there were no taxes and the battle fleet had to be laid up, which precipitated a final disaster, a brilliantly executed Dutch raid on Chatham and Sheerness in which they destroyed one of the dockyards, burnt a number of ships, and carried off the flagship, the *Royal Charles*, as a prize. To escape Impeachment, Clarendon fled abroad, there to write before he died his immortal *History of the Great Rebellion*.

In these eight years the joyous note of the Restoration had been lost for good. For England's commercial and imperial expansion it was necessary to defeat the Dutch, who had seized much of the Portuguese East Indian empire and monopolised most of the world's carrying trade. Parliament and King each blamed the other for the failure to do so; Parliament believing that the large permanent income and substantial special sums for the war which they had voted had been wasted and misapplied; the King, knowing that he had thrown into the war far more than had ever been voted, including the proceeds of the sale of Dunkirk and his Portuguese Queen's enormous dowry, putting his failure down to Parliament's meanness. Both were partly right. Thanks to the ruin of London's trade, less than half the amounts voted had in fact been collected; but of this, much had been wasted by the incompetence and corruption of government servants.

In consequence a fresh series of quarrels between King and Parliament lasted off and on to the end of the reign. The over-mighty power of Louis XIV of France, threatening all his smaller neighbours and representing the last wave of persecuting Catholicism, provoked another great outburst of anti-Catholic hysteria, and in exploiting this situation Charles tried to be too clever. He sought to avoid the stranglehold on finance and policy threatened by Parliament by selling his neutrality, or even alliance, to Louis. If Parliament would not pay him adequately to join Protestant Holland against the French, he would make Louis pay him to fight on the other side, which would also bring solid commercial advantages to England.

For a time this game was successful. By the Secret Treaties of Dover in 1670 and several subsidy agreements thereafter he got enough French money to prevent Parliament dictating his foreign policy. But Louis insisted in return that he should not only get toleration for English Catholics, but should ultimately make Catholicism his own and the nation's religion. Charles tried for the toleration, which he wanted anyway, with his Declaration of

Indulgence of 1672, and provoked such a storm that he had to surrender abjectly to Parliament and even accept a Test Act which excluded Catholics, including James, his brother and heir, from public life altogether. The growing suspicion culminated in the Popish Plot in 1678, fabricated by Shaftesbury, the republican leader, to stampede an hysterical nation into excluding James from the succession in favour of a weak-willed nominee of his own—Charles's good-looking, popular, illegitimate son, the Duke of Monmouth. Against a background of bitter faction fights in Parliament some thirty-five innocent Catholics were judicially murdered. But Charles saved the succession for his brother, and it was Shaftesbury who was ruined, so that the reign ended in 1685 in a peaceful royalist calm of reaction.

This calm did not, however, long survive the accession of the Catholic James II, who was stupid and obstinate and without political sense. In three short years he outraged every English prejudice by trying to Catholicise the whole of public life, and even the Church of England. A rebellion of the south-west on behalf of Monmouth, which ended in disastrous defeat at Sedgemoor, gave him an excuse for keeping an army full of Catholic Irish soldiers and officers. He dug out an old prerogative allowing him to dispense individuals from the operation of any particular law and dispensed Catholics wholesale from the Test Act and all the Penal Laws. Catholics filled the Council and the public service and commanded both army and fleet. Mass was everywhere publicly celebrated. Colleges at Oxford and Cambridge were perverted to Catholic seminaries, and Catholics were even appointed to the Deanery of Christ Church and the Bishopric of Oxford. Finally, by two Declarations of Indulgence, he suspended the laws against Catholics altogether; and the second was to be read aloud from every pulpit in the land.

During the Popish Plot there had emerged the beginnings of political parties: out of Shaftesbury's highly organised anti-Catholic and anti-monarchical Green Ribbon Club a group who called themselves Whigs and stood basically for the supremacy of Parliament; from among their opponents the Tories, heirs to the old Cavaliers, who stood for Church and King and held rebellion a sin as well as a crime. The Whigs would gladly have been rid of James II right from the start. But nobody wanted another civil war, and as long as the Tories stood by their doctrine of "Non-Resistance" to royal authority, James might survive, especially as he was old and his two daughters, Mary and Anne, were sound Anglicans. This last hope perished when James's second wife produced a son in June 1688 who would certainly be brought up a Catholic; and Tory loyalty collapsed altogether when their Church was ordered to collaborate in her own destruction. Seven bishops, royalist to a man, petitioned against the Declaration of Indulgence, were prosecuted by an infuriated King for sedition, and acquitted amid tremendous rejoicings, bonfires, and bell-ringing. That evening seven leading men of both parties sent an official invitation to William of Orange to come over from Holland and save English Protestantism.

William was half a Stuart and was married to James's daughter Mary. His life's work was to fight Louis XIV, and for this England would be invaluable, provided that he did not land himself in an English civil war as well. Once sure of the support of both parties he set sail and landed in Torbay in the autumn of 1688. After a momentary hesitation all England rose to greet him, and James did not even made a fight of it. Obsessed too late by the fear of ending like his father on the scaffold, he fled to France; and with him and his infant son there departed for ever the old monarchy built up by the Tudors, for which Charles I had died. Whatever constitutional arrangements might be made, no one could ever claim again to sit on the English throne by divine right. English sovereigns would henceforth be nominees of Parliament with clearly defined rights and power limited by known laws.

THE HANOVERIANS AND THE HOUSE OF WINDSOR

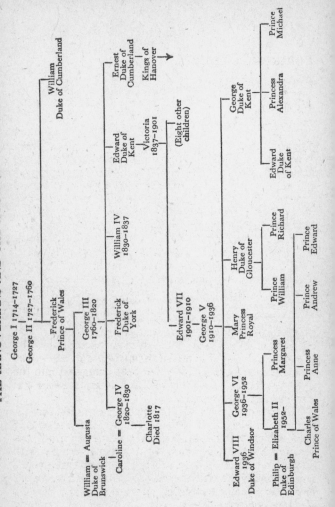

CHAPTER X

Political Stability
Economic Revolution
1688 – 1782

THOUGH the expulsion of the universally unpopular James II had been easy, it was some years before what Whigs liked to call the "Glorious, Bloodless Revolution" was complete. Lord Dundee raised the Highlands for the old Scottish dynasty, and only his death in his own victorious charge at Killiecrankie prevented a long struggle in Scotland. Catholic Ireland presented even greater difficulties, for James landed there in 1689 with 7,000 French troops, and it was a year before the relief of the loyal Protestant city of Londonderry and William's victory at the Battle of the Boyne reduced the Irish to a sullen obedience. Meanwhile, after endless wrangling in Parliament, the crown had been settled jointly on William and Mary, with Anne as the next heir. Too late many Tories bitterly regretted the change and there were constant Jacobite plots on James's behalf and, later, that of his son, the Old Pretender. But most consoled themselves with the legend that the baby born in 1688 had been smuggled into the Queen's room in a warming-pan, and accepted Mary and Anne as rightful heiresses.

The details of the new arrangements were worked out in the Bill of Rights of 1689 and the Act of Settlement of 1701, which together are the only written form of constitution England ever had. All the points disputed with Stuart kings since 1603 were finally settled in Parliament's favour; and, since William had no children and all Anne's died, the ultimate succession was vested in the Electors of Hanover, who descended from James I's daughter Elizabeth and the Elector Palatine. Mary took little part in politics and died in 1694. William III died in 1702 and Anne in 1714. After that the most diehard Tory could not pretend that divine-right monarchy survived in England. George of Hanover sat on the throne as George I by Act of Parliament alone : and sovereignty had really passed to the tax-voting House of Commons.

The years from 1688 to 1714 thus represented a sort of transition between Stuart and Georgian England. There were fierce faction fights in Parliament, the last echoes of Stuart battles as Tory squires bitterly resisted the heavy taxes which William demanded for his French wars, while in the coffee-houses, or over choice cups of the newly imported beverage of tea, an increasingly elegant London society discussed the political satires of Swift and Defoe and the essays of Addison and Steele. Out of the splendid last flowering of the English renaissance presided over by Sir Christoper Wren there grew the charming Queen Anne houses, forerunners of the Palladian mansions which embodied the Whig supremacy of the 18th century. Small capitalists were beginning to ride round the country with trains of pack horses distributing raw wool to a growing population of weavers, so laying the foundations of the large-scale organisation and expansion of industry which was to constitute the Industrial Revolution. Yet Queen Anne still touched those sick of the King's Evil and the idea of divine right was not quite dead.

Both in politics and commerce the decisive factor throughout both these reigns was the war against France. William, as a Dutchman, had only taken on the trying task of governing England to add her men and money to the alliance he was building up to save his country from being overrun by Louis XIV. Though luckless, he was a brave and dogged soldier, and by the Peace of Ryswick in 1697 he had at least halted the French advance. In 1700, however, Louis could not resist a chance to put his grandson on the Spanish throne and William had to forge another grand alliance to save Europe from French domination. He died before the war broke out, but England was already committed, thanks to Louis's support for the Old Pretender and the vital importance of trade with Spain and her colonies. For the first time since the Hundred Years' War the nation was involved in large-scale continental operations; and only the English commander, the great Duke of Marlborough, had the tact, charm and intelligence to hold the awkward alliance together. He made it a brilliant success, winning spectacular victories at Blenheim, Ramillies, Oudenarde, and Malplaquet, and by 1710 had laid the foundations of a new English military tradition. There were, furthermore, some useful strategic colonial gains at the Treaty of Utrecht in 1713; Gibraltar and Minorca, Newfoundland and Nova Scotia, and the monopoly of the profitable slave trade with South America.

All this had required an unprecedented financial effort. William spent four times as much as Charles II, and much of it had to be borrowed. Fortunately, thanks to the prosperity of the great trading companies like the East India and the African Companies, there was plenty of capital seeking investment. Nearly the whole modern system of joint-stock banking grew out of the need to organise the government's borrowing, and the Bank of England emerged as the controlling influence in the City of London, while there was already by 1713 no possibility of repaying the National Debt, which had reached £50 millions. There emerged, too, a much more defined grouping of the two parties in Parliament. The Whigs, descendants politically of the men who resisted Stuart divine right, became the war party, and absorbed into their ranks almost all the City men who profited by lending money to the government at high war rates of interest, while the Tories drew their most massive support from the landed squires who hated Land Tax at 4s. in the £ and wanted peace at any price.

The bitter opposition of these two groups might have broken out in another civil war when Queen Anne died in 1714 had Bolingbroke, the Tory leader, been ready with his plan to bring back the exiled Stuarts instead of the unprepossessing George I, whom nobody really wanted. But the Whigs got their man in first and Bolingbroke fled abroad; and a brief flurry of Jacobite rebellion in the north in 1715 ended in two half-hearted battles at Sheriffmuir and Preston. The only important result was the Septennial Act which, to avoid a general election in the middle of the crisis, prolonged the life of the existing, and future, Parliaments to seven years. The truth was that men feared that the Stuarts might repudiate the debts of William and Anne and were loath to risk their growing prosperity for any cause, however glamorous, especially since the Pretender was just as much a foreigner as George I and a Catholic into the bargain.

There was a confused period of adjustment from 1714 to 1721 while politics and commerce adapted themselves to a new world. The more extreme Tories became Jacobites. The rest raged impotently in and out of Parliament at an England which had no longer any use for their conception of Church and King. Power passed permanently to the Whigs : a combination of great landowners, merchants, bankers, and nonconformists which monopolised government at all levels. George I spoke no English and could not preside over his own Council, which henceforth met independently and became the 'Cabinet'; and out of the squabbles of the various Whig groups there emerged in 1721 the stable power of Sir Robert Walpole who, by a mixture of ability and bribery and by the clever use of government patronage in Church, army, and civil service and the manipulation of groups in the Commons, kept together a Parliamentary majority until 1742, and in doing so became the first Prime Minister, though it was then a term of abuse and not an official appointment.

Walpole succeeded to power at a very happy moment. Differences with Spain over the trading clauses of the Treaty of Utrecht had all but led to a renewal of general war, and Admiral Byng did actually sink the Spanish Mediterranean fleet off Cape Passaro in 1718. Financial inexperience had also produced a crisis in the City, when a wave of speculation culminated in the crash of the heavily over-capitalised South Sea Company. Numbers of other companies, many of them totally fraudulent—one was for "a certain design which will hereafter be promulgated"—crashed with it. Thousands of families were ruined and one Cabinet minister was so deeply implicated that he shot himself. Twenty-one years of stability and peaceful prosperity were just what England needed, and Walpole with his famous motto of "Let sleeping dogs lie" was just the man to provide it.

There was as yet no large industrialisation of England, nor any very rapid increase of population. Here and there, in the expansion of Tyneside coal-mining operations and the enlargement of some factory workshops, there were signs of future development; and Walpole's brother-in-law, Lord Townshend, retired from politics in 1730 to make the experiments with root crops which were soon to revolutionise agriculture. But England's wealth was still mainly commercial. Newfoundland fisheries, the sugar exports of Barbados, worth all the exports of the other American colonies put together, the Hudson's Bay Company's rich hauls of furs, and the cargoes of luxuries which poured in from the East Indies, were the sources of the prosperity so carefully nursed by Walpole. Almost his only positive act—the Molasses Act of 1733—was a concession to the powerful sugar magnates. His Excise Scheme, defeated by stupid and factious opposition, was designed to free more trade, and he thought always in terms of the merchant interest. Mostly he just governed, and in twenty years the value of English exports doubled.

Nothing, however, was done for the poor. The Molasses Act kept sugar dear and the Salt Tax was deliberately retained to ease the burden of Land Tax on the richer classes. Parliament refused to tax the profits on spirits, though cheap gin was the main cause of London's atrocious death rate. In London, indeed, social conditions were never worse than during this period. Elsewhere the old Tudor parish system still worked, creakily but adequately. The sprawling growth of London in spite of the fact that there were three deaths there for every birth, threw on to the handful of magistrates, constables, and Poor Law overseers impossible problems which they mostly abandoned in despair. A vicious, hopeless, diseased, gin-sodden, and increasingly criminal population were huddled in alleys and unpaved streets of hovels unpoliced, without churches, schools, hospitals, workhouses, or the most elementary sanitation, and for years the only government contribution was to increase the number of capital offences, which achieved nothing save a few more hangings.

By the end of Walpole's administration individual philanthropy was beginning slightly to relieve the situation. Five of London's great hospitals had been founded, and a high duty on gin after 1751 brought the death rate down spectacularly; and the drafting of herds of unwanted children by harassed and powerless overseers to die as virtually slave labour in Spitalfields silk factories or northern mills and mines was checked by proper regulations for feeding and boarding them in the country. But on the whole Walpole's Georgian England, calm and spacious, elegant and immensely rich, complacently ignored London's poor. Kindly and patriarchal enough to their own country dependants, the landlords were not aware of the capital as a responsibility, and the Church was sinking, too, into a Georgian calm. Amiable as he was, Walpole was no man to lead a crusade. His policy served the needs of those who controlled votes.

The commercial interests which profited from this Sabbath calm also brought it to an end. The death of George II's Queen, Caroline, in 1737 greatly weakened Walpole's position. It was her friendship which had kept him in office when her peppery and rather stupid soldier husband succeeded in 1727 and in the usual Hanoverian way proposed to dismiss all his father's ministers. Without her he could not resist the merchant clamour for war to open up the Spanish American market in 1739, which quickly involved the country in the general War of the Austrian Succession; and behind that there was a quarrel with France, also rooted in commercial and colonial considerations. The English had colonised the coast of North America. The French threatened, by joining up with a chain of forts their settlements in Canada and Louisiana to block all further expansion inland by these one and a half million English. In India the rival East India Companies were fighting out a private war with untold wealth at

THE FIGHT FOR THE
AMERICA COLONIES

Hudson's Bay

CANADA

The Great Lakes

Quebec

R. St. Lawrence

Montreal

NEW ENGLAND

NEW YORK

Saratoga

Boston

PENNSYLVANIA

R. Ohio

Alleghany

VIRGINIA

Yorktown

R. Missouri

R. Tennessee

CAROLINA

ATLANTIC OCEAN

LOUISIANA

GEORGIA

R. Mississippi

FLORIDA

French Colonies
underlined
Proposed line of French forts
✗✗✗✗✗✗

100   0   100   200 Miles

stake in which, too, the governments were bound to get involved.

Walpole turned out to be a very bad war minister; and so the era of peace and government by one man gave way to one of wars conducted by Whig groups—what they called 'Broad Bottomed' administration. The fighting in all three theatres of war was evenly balanced. The capture of Louisburg in Canada was offset by the loss of Madras in India. In Europe George II was present to see his troops win at Dettingen in 1743, but the French revenged themselves at Fontenoy two years later. As a distraction in that same year, 1745, the French sent the Stuart Young Pretender, Charles Edward, to Scotland, and for a moment the Hanoverian succession seemed really threatened. Scottish Jacobitism had been largely nourished by hatred of England ever since the two countries had been formally united in 1707, and at first Prince Charlie carried all before him. His invasion of England, however, though he got to Derby and caused a panic in London, failed because men were too well satisfied with their dividends to indulge in romantic adventures and in any case were terrified of his Highlanders. He turned back, and in due course the Duke of Cumberland caught and defeated him at Culloden. The Prince got away after a series of legendary escapes, and Cumberland—Sweet William to the English florists—earned his Scottish nickname of 'Butcher' by the brutality of his revenge.

There was official peace in 1748, with all conquests handed back, but fighting never really stopped, and general war soon flared up again, disastrously for England. By 1757, when William Pitt, Earl of Chatham, took over the government from the incompetent Duke of Newcastle, Admiral Byng had lost Minorca, and very unjustly been shot for it, two vital forts had been lost in America, and 123 Britons had been massacred in the Black Hole of Calcutta, while Cumberland had been forced to withdraw from Europe altogether. A clerk named Clive saved the Indian situation, winning a great victory against overwhelming odds at Plassey, from which the French power and influence never recovered. Elsewhere Chatham's dynamic energy and ability to pick good men turned the scale. The year of victories, 1759, saw the French defeated at sea at Quiberon and Lagos, in Europe at Minden, and in America at Ticonderoga and Quebec.

A new King in 1760, George III, quickly got rid of the gouty, insufferably ill-tempered Chatham and substituted a series of incompetent administrations of his own friends the last of which, under Lord North, by quarrelling with the American colonists, endangered all that Chatham had won. The colonies were not well governed and there was certainly exploitation for the benefit of English merchants and manufacturers. They were denied free trade, and they paid large sums in indirect taxation to the British government without having what the House of Commons itself had fought so hard to win the century before, representation of their grievances and a vote on taxation. On the other hand, the Americans, too, had their profitable monopolies in the English market—tobacco for example—and it was not unreasonable that they should be asked to contribute to their own very costly defence by a British fleet and army. Furthermore, much of their clamour against tariffs was undoubtedly that of frustrated smugglers.

Tact and statesmanship in London might have healed the whole dispute, as Chatham pointed out in a dying speech in the House of Lords. Instead, a bullying, assertive policy brought out all the sturdy resentment of men most of whose ancestors had emigrated in great hardship and danger to escape religious or political tyranny. In 1776 the situation was allowed to drift into open war; and, thanks again to governmental incompetence, George Washington's fluctuating, independable forces of insubordinate and untrained volunteers more than held their own against the regular army. When, through sheer War Office muddle, General Burgoyne was forced to surrender with 4,000 men at Saratoga in 1777, the French joined in to seek their revenge and were allowed to gain temporary command at sea. Thus when, in 1781, General Cornwallis fell back on the coast at Yorktown he found a French instead of an English fleet, and yet another British army had to surrender. A year later Rodney recovered naval supremacy by his brilliant victory at the Saints, but the war and the empire Chatham had saved was lost. American independence had to be recognised, and only Canada remained to give Englishmen a chance to show that they could learn from their mistakes.

Not even George III could keep North in office after this, and out of the confusion that followed his fall there emerged in 1783 the second great Prime Minister of the century, Chatham's twenty-four-year-old younger son, William Pitt. By then the task of reconstruction which had to be faced was formidable. The House of Commons and the whole Whig system had lost sadly in prestige during the corruptions and scandals of the past twenty years. At home as well as in America ministers had tried to assert arbitrary powers such as their ancestors had denied to Charles I, and there had been a major struggle over the right to arrest and search under general warrants. They had been defeated by a disreputable aristocrat named Wilkes who got himself elected four times for Middlesex and was each time expelled as unfit to sit. When, on the fifth occasion, the Commons declared his opponent elected in the teeth of the votes, Wilkes turned out the London mob and, to the cry of "Wilkes and Liberty", forced the government to give way, incidentally establishing in the course of the struggle the important right to have the debates of Parliament reported to the public. In 1780 there had been more trouble of a different sort, when government indecision let London lie for days at the mercy of the anti-Catholic Gordon rioters. But these troubles were as nothing to the problems raised by the first beginnings of the industrial revolution.

All the necessary elements were now at last present. Townshend's turnips had not only vastly improved the rotation of crops, but had made it possible to keep and fatten stock over the winter, and had so led to selective breeding which was doubling the size of cattle and sheep. Progressive methods, demanding capital and large-scale farming, led in turn to the enclosure of seven million acres —almost all that remained—of the common and waste land, so that, one way or another, England could feed five times as many people as before, and for this reason alone a falling death rate brought a rise in population. Moreover, a fresh flood of dispossessed smallholders filled the towns, swelling the mass of unskilled labour seeking employment; and commercial prosperity had provided plenty of capital to exploit it. A more prosperous Europe offered an almost unlimited market for cheap manufactured goods. The supply of raw materials beneath the earth or in the cotton-fields of America seemed inexhaustible.

The mechanical inventions which would enable this to be usefully applied were still in their infancy and, until transport improved enough to enable large quantities of coal and iron to be moved about the country, progress would be slow. But the Earl of Bridgewater and his engineer, Brindley, had begun to construct the canals which would partially solve this problem; and Kay's flying shuttle in 1738 had speeded up hand-loom weaving and created a demand for more yarn which Arkwright and Crompton had met with their inventions of the Spinning Jenny and Mule, harnessing water-power to spinning and so increasing output a hundredfold. Meanwhile methods had been found to smelt iron in blast furnaces heated by coal, and by 1769 James Watt had produced the first efficient steam engine.

The developments resulting from all this were still in their infancy, and the huge aggregations of industrial manpower in factory areas round the sources of power and raw material had scarcely begun. But already there was a growth and shift of the population which put intolerable strains, as it had earlier in London, on an administrative system fundamentally unchanged since the Tudors. The population of Yorkshire and Lancashire was doubled and was beginning to be grouped round the mills dotted along the rivers which drove them. The value of raw cotton imports rose from £3 million in 1750 to over £20 million by 1780. This alone made a thorough overhaul of the machinery of government essential and rendered the system of representation in Parliament quite out of date. The sparse population of Cornwall still returned 44 members to Parliament; Manchester, already with 30,000 inhabitants, sent none at all. There were rotten boroughs all over the country where scarcely an inhabitant remained and the local landowner merely nominated the member, and there were many more where the number of voters was so small that it was only too easy to bribe or coerce them. In the counties the vote was still restricted to those who owned land freehold of the value of at least 40s. a year, though thanks to enclosure the typical farmer was now the prosperous tenant of some large estate. Municipal governments were even worse: corrupt systems for the most part, last overhauled in the reign of Charles II, and since much decayed. All this and more would demand Pitt's attention if the gains of the previous century were not to be lost in confusion and revolution.

CHAPTER XI

Reform and Reaction
The Napoleonic Wars
1782 – 1822

GEORGE III had called Pitt to office largely to keep out Charles James Fox, his brilliant but erratic rival, whom the king detested. He found that he had overreached himself, for Pitt turned out extremely autocratic, was firmly master in his own Cabinet, and refused all royal interference in policy. Since, with one brief interruption, he remained in office for over twenty years, he finally fixed the pattern of English government vested in a united and indivisible Cabinet presided over by one man, as foreshadowed by Walpole. At the same time the intermittent, and finally permanent insanity of the King completed the elimination of the Crown from the day-to-day business of politics.

But, though Pitt was a tyrant within his Cabinet and ruthless in his dealings with George III, he could never quite command the permanent majority in the House of Commons needed to push through whole-hearted reform. The old Whig system, by which each magnate brought his group of members to the support of the government, was still too powerful; and too many of the Whig grandees were entirely satisfied still with what had been achieved in 1688 and saw no need for change. Pitt was not the sort of man of principle to resign office if he could not find a majority for some measure he believed in. In general he preferred to drop the measure and stay in office. He achieved, therefore, what he could rather than what he knew ought to be done. Moreover, the French Revolution threw all plans for reform out of focus in 1789, and from

1792 onwards a fresh series of wars with France forced the abandonment of the whole programme.

None the less, the achievement of the years 1783-9 was impressive and, as it turned out, just sufficient to enable England to fight off the French without herself succumbing to revolution. The most important reforms were economic; and here Pitt had the advantage of having read and understood the work of the first great economic thinker, George Adam Smith. The situation which he found on taking office was very bad. With the American colonies England had lost a third of her overseas trade, and the wars had pushed the National Debt up to £238 millions. Working through a reorganised Board of Trade, Pitt at once set about reducing customs duties and rationalising the whole tariff system, which was chaotic; and he pushed through Walpole's abandoned Excise Scheme. Since England had no competion to fear in the market for her cheap manufactures, the move towards free trade was instantly and wholly beneficial. The volume of trade was quickly restored and soon surpassed. Customs revenue steadily increased in spite of the lowered duties; and it was possible to start a Sinking Fund by which, had not the French wars intervened, the National Debt would have been completely wiped out by 1813. At the same time stringent commissions of enquiry into government spending, regular audits, and the practice of putting government loans out to tender instead of using high rates of interest to bribe votes in the House of Commons, saved so much money that it was possible in ten years to rebuild the battle fleet out of the ordinary revenue.

This restoration of financial confidence and the greatly expanded volume of export trade which resulted from it alone sufficed to alleviate the worst effects of the sudden industrial expansion which was beginning. In a world of full employment the only victims at first were those craftsmen who became redundant when machines replaced their labour; and though this often and inevitably caused much misery, it was generally localised in one industry at a time and only temporary in its effects. Even this might have been somewhat relieved had Pitt's administrative reforms penetrated down to the local government level. At the centre he was brilliantly successful, substituting at last proper salaries and pensions in place of many of the ramshackle Jacobean perquisites and sinecures which had produced every sort of anomaly; so that few men were paid for what they actually did, and the largest rewards went to those who did nothing, but were politically valuable. Even this was not complete when the Revolution ended Pitt's era of reform, and there was no redistribution of the county and borough administration at all. The old system, already out of date and cracking under the strain, was left quite unreformed to take the full shock of the big industrial changes and the coming rapid growth and shift of the population.

In his larger legislative plans Pitt was less successful. He did pass an India Act to bring the East India Company's political activities under government control, since it was insufferable that a body of City merchants should be in a position to plunge the whole nation into an expensive war. But his sweeping plan for Parliamentary Reform was defeated by conservative vested interests in the Commons. The same happened to Wilberforce's Bill, which Pitt sponsored, to abolish the Slave Trade; and though he imposed death duties to lift some of the burden of taxation from the poor, Parliament would not have them levied on land.

The French Revolution put an end to this hopeful and adventurous period. English reaction to it was at first uncertain. Of the Whigs, who constituted not only the government majority but also the bulk of the opposition, the more liberal, led by Fox, hailed the fall of the Bastille and the Declaration of Liberty, Equality, and Fraternity in Paris as a great emancipation which they expected to bring France into line with Britain. The more conservative, inspired by the essays and speeches of Edmund Burke, saw at once a threat to order and property everywhere. However enthusiastically the revolutionaries proclaimed the brotherhood of man and renounced all foreign conquest, ideas so universal were bound to cross frontiers and rouse the hostility of the despotic governments of Europe. French patriotism became identified with the new ideas which, as they spread, brought French armies behind them, united in a crusading fervour.

At the same time the Paris mob, mobilised and led by the extremists of the Jacobin Club, rapidly eliminated the moderates who might indeed, have established something not unlike the England of 1688, and by the Terror and the guillotine forced every Frenchman to declare for the Revolution. The King and Queen were executed and every vestige of the old régime was swept away. Propertied and prosperous Whigs, devoted though they were to freedom and representative institutions, were far from being democrats or wanting the political emancipation of the masses. Fox's Revolutionary Society which corresponded with the Paris clubs and toasted the Revolution, dropped rapidly out of fashion, until Fox and a faithful handful who persisted in their liberalism constituted the whole of the Parliamentary opposition which, it was mockingly said, could be carried to the House in a couple hackney carriages. Pitt and the vast majority of Lords and Commons moved into Burke's camp, becoming over the next twenty years a new Tory party pledged, not to Church and King, but to the established order of things, and bitterly hostile to sweeping change of any kind.

Though halted abruptly in his schemes for reform, Pitt still hoped for three years to keep Englishmen 'spectators' merely of French struggles. The invasion and annexation of Belgium by the revolutionary government put an end to that. It was a British axiom that no potentially hostile great power should be allowed in the Low Countries : The Scheldt estuary, Pitt said, was a pistol pointed at England's heart. Moreover, the war had become one of ideas. The French were now threatening the freedom of the rest of Europe as clearly as had the Catholicism of Philip of Spain and the aggressive nationalism of Louis XIV. It was, as Pitt said, 'armed opinion' which had to be fought; and in an obscure, muddled way England agreed with him. Men who did not think politically at all—even seamen trapped into serving their country by the press gang —were deeply, if not very logically convinced for the next twenty years that they were fighting to keep England and Europe free.

The course of events in France and Europe in the end proved them fundamentally right. The Revolution evolved in due course to the inevitable end of all such movements in a military dictatorship. France's most successful general, Napoleon Bonaparte, seized power as 'First Consul' in 1799, and five years later made himself Emperor. The conquest of Belgium was followed by that of Holland, by the invasion of Italy and of Egypt. France achieved the ambition of centuries—the Rhine frontier—and made it clear that even that was not enough. From 1793 onwards Britain alone consistently opposed her, and, except for a short break under the Treaty of Amiens in 1802 the war was continuous until 1814.

For thirteen years Pitt showed himself a not very competent war minister. His method was sound enough : to make his main effort at sea and use Britain's huge wealth to subsidise continental coalitions to bear the brunt of the land fighting. But the coalitions could not stand up to the enthusiasm of the French armies or Napoleon's military genius, and Pitt lacked his father's flair for spotting the decisive theatre and sending the right man to operate in it. But he kept England in the war with dogged courage and persistence and worked himself to death in the process.

At sea, thanks to the rebuilt fleet and the reorganisation of signalling and tactics by a group of brilliant young officers who had fought under Rodney at the Saints, England more than held her own. It took time to perfect the system of blockade which was in the end to have a crippling effect on the French effort, and though Lord Howe won his battle on the Glorious First of June in 1794, he failed to prevent the French grain convoy getting into Brest harbour. Naval mutinies revealed grave deficiencies in pay and conditions, and only bad weather prevented the French from invading Ireland in 1796. But in 1797, when the Spanish and Dutch fleets were put at the disposal of the enemy, Duncan destroyed the Dutch at Camperdown and Jervis defeated the Spaniards at Cape St. Vincent, where a young captain named Nelson made his name.

From then on the admirals controlled the situation, penning the French fleets in their ports and slowly strangling all Europe's overseas trade; and, when Napoleon broke out to invade Egypt in 1798, as a stepping-stone to India, Nelson sank his fleet in Aboukir Bay, and he had to leave his army behind there to be defeated in due course by General Abercromby.

The blockade had its disadvantages. By cutting off Europe's luxuries it created much discontent and enabled Napoleon in 1801 to unite Russia, Prussia, Denmark and Sweden in an Armed Neutrality against England. Nelson again dealt with that, and kept the Baltic open by destroying the Danish fleet at Copenhagen. But Pitt's coalitions had not been able to stand up to the French who by 1802 could dictate terms to Europe. English military strength had been dissipated in futile, costly expeditions against Toulon and in the West Indies; and the main effort in Flanders, under the King's second son, the Duke of York, which ought to have helped the Prussians and Austrians to capture Paris, did little except a lot of marching best commemorated in the nursery rhyme about "the good old Duke of York". Amiens was a peace of exhaustion, from which we gained only Ceylon and Trinidad to offset a new debt of £290 millions.

Worse still, a century of misgovernment and neglect in Ireland had come home to roost in 1798, incidentally forcing Pitt temporarily out of office. The Catholic peasants were exasperated by the corrupt political monopoly of the Anglo-Protestants and by absentee landlords who spent the rents racked from them in Bath or on the grand tour. The Scots-descended Presbyterian farmers of the north were equally aggrieved by the same sort of fiscal policy as had alienated the American colonists. To tide over the crisis of the American war the Irish Parliament had been made independent, but it remained exclusively Protestant and incurably corrupt, and Pitt was not allowed to extend most of his free-trade measures to Ireland. French revolutionary ideas, on top of American emancipation, spread fast, especially in the north, and in the south there was the traditional feeling that England's crisis was Ireland's opportunity.

The resulting '98 rebellion was feeble and ill-organised. But it pinned down 45,000 troops badly needed elsewhere and it convinced Pitt that Ireland, like Scotland, would be better ruled from Westminster. Bribery on an unprecedented scale induced the Irish Parliament to vote itself out of existence, and Ireland was promised Catholic Emancipation in exchange for her independence. Unfortunately George III, temporarily sane but incurably stupid and obstinate, would not let Pitt keep his bargain, holding that to free the Catholics from their disabilities would be a breach of his Anglican coronation oath. Pitt saved his personal honour by resigning, but this did not console the Irish, who were left with one more great betrayal to add to a long list.

In consequence England faced one of the greatest threats in her history with the feeble Addington at the head of a quarrelling and incompetent government. Napoleon used the short peace to continue preparations for an attack on England which should open his way to India; and England for her part could never be reconciled to the hegemony in Europe of a French military dictator. The fight to the death between the two opened in May 1803, with the whole of the European coastline garrisoned by the French and the tents of the invasion army of 160,000 men clearly visible in fine weather across the Channel at Boulogne. Feverish and slightly futile preparations were being made to meet the threat. Martello observation towers sprang up all along the south coast. Plans were made to evacuate Parliament and the Bank of England; and everywhere hastily raised militia regiments drilled and exercised enthusiastically in the rather forlorn hope of defeating the finest veteran army Europe had ever seen. The crisis brought Pitt back to office in 1804, and he at once set about another coalition to relieve the pressure. But in the last analysis it all turned on the seamen. Napoleon somewhat optimistically demanded from his admirals only twenty-four hours uninterrupted use of the Channel. Lord Barham at the Admiralty and the fleet commanders afloat were imperturbably certain that he could not get even that.

The crisis came in the spring of 1805, when Admiral Villeneuve evaded Nelson's blockade of Toulon. But even when he had picked up the Spanish fleet and decoyed Nelson on a long chase to the West Indies he still could not break into the Channel to pick up the Rochefort and Brest fleets, and he put back into Cadiz. From that moment Napoleon's plan was doomed. He decided at once to go east for a back door to destroy British power, and so provoked the two most decisive events of the war. Villeneuve, coming out to break through into the Mediterranean, met Nelson at Trafalgar to give England the most legendary of all her victories and a control of the seas henceforth unchallengeable. Nelson, who captured the English imagination as nobody else since Alfred, was killed, and his dying boast in the cockpit of the *Victory* that he had done his duty was literally true. He had made England invulnerable. But Napoleon's lightning dash to destroy the Austrians at Austerlitz made him the equally invincible master of Europe. Land and sea power now faced each other in an apparent deadlock.

Austerlitz killed Pitt. For a short space he was replaced by a coalition of "All the Talents", which gave Fox the chance for his one creative achievement, the abolition of the Slave Trade. After that, government devolved on a series of nonentities dominated from the Foreign Office by Lord Castlereagh. The French struggle meanwhile became an economic and diplomatic tug-of-war in which England slowly gained the advantage. Napoleon, thinking to break a "nation of shopkeepers" by bankruptcy, closed every port in Europe to British goods by his Berlin Decrees, and Britain countered with Orders in Council aimed to cut off Europe's overseas imports altogether. There were, indeed, many individual bankruptcies and there was much defeatism in London, while the Americans, exasperated by losing their European market, declared war in 1812. But Napoleon was the loser. He could not hold down a Europe deprived of almost all its luxuries. To enforce his decrees he had to invade first Spain and

Portugal, so giving England the chance to open the "running sore" of the Peninsular War, and then Russia, which ruined him.

The Peninsular War perfectly demonstrated how effective amphibious operations could be even against overwhelming land forces. Napoleon himself at the head of 200,000 men had his whole Spanish invasion disrupted by Sir John Moore's small force cutting across his communications and slipping back to embark at Corunna. The War Office still hankered after Belgian operations, and in 1809 another 40,000 men were sent to die of disease at Walcheren. But there were just enough men and supplies left to keep Sir Arthur Wellesley, in due course Duke of Wellington, entrenched in Portugal behind the Lines of Torres Vedras, well fed by the fleet, while the French slowly starved on the meagre surplus of Spain. Battle by battle Wellington wore down their strength until, at Vittoria in 1813, he destroyed it altogether. By then Napoleon's disastrous retreat from Moscow had enabled Castlereagh to form the last and greatest coalition in which almost all Europe combined to force the Emperor slowly back to Paris and, in 1814, to abdicate; and by then Wellington was fighting at Toulouse, deep in the heart of France.

After twenty-five years of war and the ceaseless rearrangement of Europe to suit Napoleon's dynastic convenience, it was not easy for the diplomats who then assembled at the Congress of Vienna to establish what Castlereagh called "peace and a just equilibrium". In fact they restored as much as possible of the situation of 1789, seeking above all to make any fresh revolutionary outbreak impossible. Since this involved much interference by the great powers in the affairs of their neighbours, Castlereagh and his successor, George Canning, steadily drifted apart from their late allies. Britain was satisfied to have kept the world's trading routes clear and to have gained a few strategic points like Malta after a war which had cost her £600 million, and she lost interest in the continent. But before this rift could develop Napoleon closed his enemies' ranks again by returning from Elba, where he had been exiled, in a last bid for power.

Such was the spell of his name that France rallied to him again and all Europe was in a panic. He had little chance of defeating the huge forces available against him, but he might by one great victory induce his exhausted enemies to leave him on the French throne. This was the threat which Wellington met and defeated at Waterloo. He had only 67,000 men against 74,000 French, and of those only 21,000 were British and few of them were Peninsular veterans, most of whom had been sent to America. For the whole of a long day he fought the Emperor off, losing a quarter of his army in killed and wounded in one of the hardest-fought battles in history; and by the time Marshal Blücher's Prussians joined the fight in the evening it was virtually over. The French broke and fled, carrying with them the Emperor whose last hope had gone; and so badly had he frightened Europe that this time he was sent to the lonely Atlantic island of St. Helena, whence there was no escape and where he died.

The damage which the war had done to England was inestimable. The danger lay not so much in the commercial losses, serious though these were, as in the unremedied abuses of 1789 which by 1815 were a thousand times more threatening. The population of about six and a half millions of 1750 had grown to eleven by 1801 and by 1831 was to be over sixteen millions. Thanks, moreover, to the rapid advance of mechanisation during the war and the improvement in transport by the extension of the canal system and by Macadam's new process of surfacing roads, the masses were becoming dangerously concentrated. Manchester's 30,000 rose to 187,000 by 1821, and the woollen industry of Yorkshire, the Staffordshire potteries and the steel foundries wherever coal and iron were easily available, had produced similar aggregations all over the midlands and the north.

These great displacements of the population and the disruption of the way of life of centuries must have produced untold misery in any event. Unsupervised by a

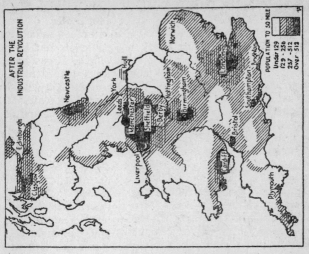

BEFORE THE
INDUSTRIAL REVOLUTION

Newcastle

York
Hull

Leeds

Liverpool

Norwich

London

Bristol

Exeter

POPULATION TO 50 MILE

Under 129
129 - 256
257 - 512

AFTER THE
INDUSTRIAL REVOLUTION

Edinburgh

Glasgow

Newcastle

York
Hull

Leeds
Manchester
Sheffield

Liverpool

Derby
Nottingham

Birmingham

Norwich

London

Cardiff

Bristol

Southampton

Brighton

Plymouth

POPULATION TO 50 MILE

Under 129
129 - 256
257 - 512
Over 512

government preoccupied with a life-and-death struggle with France, its effects were almost indescribable. There was no law to enforce safety and sanitary conditions in factory or mine, or to protect workers and their children from unlimited exploitation in overcrowded labour markets; no local authority to provide drains or to restrict the jerry builder; no magistrate or police to enforce what law there was; no churches, schools, or hospitals at all. In fact everything which had been almost intolerable in 1780 had become entirely so by 1815. The worst conditions in London earlier in the century were now reproduced in a hundred new industrial towns where the houses went up back to back and the drainage seeped through the unpaved streets into cellars, every one of which housed a teeming family.

Two factors combined to make things much worse than they need have been. One was the fashionable economic theory of *laissez-faire* which taught that all interference with the laws of supply and demand could only make things worse; that nature must be left to redress her own balances, and that population would always rise to subsistence level, so that any attempt at remedy would merely produce more people to starve. In consequence many whose consciences rebelled at industrial conditions felt themselves powerless to help. The other was the wartime mentality which regarded any protest by workers as unpatriotic or revolutionary. Habeas Corpus was suspended in 1794. The Gagging Acts of 1795 forbade meetings of more than fifty persons without a magistrate's licence; and the Combination Laws made any workers' club, union, or friendly society illegal for fear that it might become Jacobin.

Inexcusably the government prolonged this repressive policy even after 1815 and all but provoked the very revolution it feared. Trade recovered fast and exports were soon twice what they had been in 1790, but the new wealth went into the pockets of factory owners, merchants, and those under whose land the coal and iron lay. The real wages of the poor have never been lower in England than at this time, nor conditions worse. Corn laws to save the farmers and landlords from foreign competition kept bread dear; and every protest, however peaceful, was met by armed force. Exasperated folk burnt ricks and smashed the machinery which was ruining their lives, and there were bands which drilled with pikes secretly at night in the hills. The climax came between 1819 and 1821, with the 'Peterloo Massacre', when panicky magistrates loosed cavalry on a peaceful gathering of 80,000 in Manchester and eleven people were killed and many injured; in the Cato Street conspiracy to assassinate the whole government; and in the Six Acts which tightened all restrictions on working men's activities and put a high stamp duty on newspapers to prevent the spread of ideas. It is small wonder that, when Castlereagh went mad and killed himself in 1822, the crowd cheered his coffin into Westminster Abbey. Their instinct, too, proved right. For with his death new men came to power who had better remedies to offer than mere repression, and with them a new era opened.

CHAPTER XII

The Second Great Crisis
The Age of Reform
1822 – 1848

CASTLEREAGH's death brought to the front a group who
have been called the Tory Reformers. Heirs of Pitt in his
pre-Revolution period, they believed the existing constitution perfectly workable if brought up to date by
administrative tinkering; and by breaking away from the
purely static conservatism of Old Tories like Wellington,
they hoped to take all the wind out of the sails of Grey
and the ex-Foxite Whigs who clamoured for wholesale
Parliamentary Reform.

This main objective they did not achieve, but their
attempt between 1822 and 1828 helped enormously to
relieve the pressure of working-class discontent. Canning,
their leader, confined his activities to the Foreign Office,
liberalising without forsaking the non-intervention policy
formulated by Castlereagh; and their largest contribution
was made by Huskisson at the Board of Trade and Robin-
son as Chancellor of the Exchequer. All the venerable
lumber of customs duties and navigation restrictions left
behind by Pitt were now systematised, and home and Irish
trade were totally freed. They left little or no duty on raw
materials, an average of 20 per cent on manufactured
goods, and by a number of valuable commercial treaties
on a basis of reciprocal concessions greatly stimulated
export trade. Only colonial goods were henceforth heavily
protected. Pursuing Pitt's policy, the two reaped Pitt's
reward of a steadily rising revenue in spite of lowered
duties. Reduced taxes still further stimulated manufactures, and a share of the rising tide of wealth inevitably
fell to the poorest classes, if only in the form of falling

prices. At the same time Sir Robert Peel at the Home Office, though his political allegiance was to the Old Tories, alleviated much misery and injustice by reforming the criminal code, abolishing the death penalty for more than a hundred offences, and giving London at last the much needed Metropolitan Police, which were to serve as a model for the whole modern world.

None of the work of these men went to the root of England's troubles, which needed something more drastic than administrative reform. But they created a world of slightly improving conditions in which men felt less goaded to violent remedies for their ills. Almost inadvertently, too, they made a very important permanent contribution by the repeal of the Combination Laws. The immediate effects of this overdue measure were disastrous. Hundreds of small unions, hastily formed by leaders without experience, organised on too narrow a basis, and without reserve funds, tried to use the strike weapon to improve wages and conditions, and were uniformly unsuccessful. The effect was to disillusion the mass of workers with industrial action as a remedy and to turn their minds instead to political reform. But the last and greatest of the strikes, when Hepburn in 1832 kept 8,000 Tyneside miners out for 23 weeks, in spite of a cholera epidemic, and without any serious disorder, though it failed, pointed the way to what might be achieved in the future. Trade Unionism had to serve a twenty-year apprenticeship before it could become effective. Meanwhile all the 50,000 who bought and the many more who read Cobbett's weekly *Political Register* were convinced that only a reformed Parliament would remedy their diverse grievances.

The Tory reform attempt was in fact foredoomed to failure. Behind Grey and the Whigs there was a mounting tide of public opinion which, though unrepresented in Parliament, could bring a massive and relentless pressure to bear on the governing class. It was not only the gangs in the countryside who burnt ricks and smashed threshing machines and the mobs which rioted and burnt down Lancashire mills, but also the respectable tradesmen and small industrialists who, now that the war was over, felt free to clamour for the vote. Tories could not really argue that the Commons still fairly represented public opinion in the teeth of the known facts of pocket boroughs and corrupt electioneering, of the great urban masses wholly unrepresented, and the unjustifiable preponderance of the landed gentry. The monarchy, too, had forfeited all respect amidst the debauches, extravagances and scandals of all George III's sons, the most disreputable of whom had been Regent since his father went mad in 1811 and since 1820 had sat on the throne as George IV: a drunken, bloated parody of the charming and elegant young man who had once been hailed as the First Gentleman of Europe. Finally, far too much of the real power seemed to rest with a block of blindly reactionary peers who regarded any expression of legitimate grievance as revolutionary agitation.

Canning's government broke up soon after his death in 1827. For two years Wellington, loyally supported by Peel, tried to fend off the clamour for reform by ignoring it, though even he felt obliged to make one great concession by passing Catholic Emancipation. This measure, also long overdue, at last allowed Catholics a full share in public life, and was intended to rob the Whigs of one of the main planks in their platform. In fact it only divided the Tories among themselves, and in 1830 Lord Grey at last secured a majority in the House of Commons in favour of Reform and forced Wellington out of office.

Most of Grey's cabinet were Lords, and there was nothing democratic in their Reform Bill, revolutionary though it seemed to the diehard Tories. They used the mounting excitement of the masses throughout the country, the rick-burnings and the riots, and the crowds shouting for "the Bill, the whole Bill, and nothing but the Bill" to frighten the Tory peers into accepting reform as a lesser evil than revolution. But they did not intend to give the vote to a single one of the working men who shouted and rioted for them. They merely wished to tidy up the existing system by abolishing 143 rotten or very underpopulated boroughs and transferring their seats to the new cities and more thickly inhabited counties. The vote was to remain firmly anchored to property; and although the richer tenant farmers were added to the 40s. freeholders as county voters, and every occupier of a house worth £10 a year got the borough vote, this only increased the total number of voters from 435,000 to 685,000.

This was, however, a sweeping measure by comparison with what Pitt had proposed, and Grey had a hard fight to make the Tory Lords and the new King, William IV, let it go through. When the Lords threw out his first Bill he had to risk the disorder of a General Election in the midst of the over-excitement; and even though he returned with a handsome majority for Reform, he still had to persuade the King to threaten the creation of fifty Whig peers before the Tories in the Lords would give in. In the end Wellington's sanity prevailed on his more sensible colleagues to let the nation have its way, however much they disapproved, and amidst tremendous rejoicing the Bill went through.

Inevitably the masses whose clamour had pushed the Bill through were bitterly disappointed with the result. Once again, as with the repeal of the Combination Laws, their radical leaders had promised them that this single measure would remedy all their ills, and once again they found themselves apparently no better off. For the worst of the discontent there was indeed nothing any government could have done but organise unemployment relief. As mechanisation spread it produced in one industry after another great blocks of unemployables : men whose skill was supplanted by machines and who were too old to learn a new craft. The uneven pace of mechanisation, even within a single industry, often made this problem worse. Spinning machinery came before weaving machinery, and so produced a boom in hand-loom weaving and a great rise in numbers to deal with the increased output of yarn. There were thus even more men to suffer disaster when power looms came into general use. These were evils only time could remedy, as industry settled into its new pattern, as the old men died, and the young were absorbed by the rising tide of prosperity.

Nevertheless the belief persisted among those who were denied the vote in 1832 that purely political reform would automatically bring about the improvements needed in industrial conditions, and their disappointment found expression over the next ten years in Chartism. The People's Charter for which they agitated was a sensible enough programme of reform, only one of whose six points was impracticable : the demand for annual general elections. The other five—secret ballot, manhood suffrage, payment of M.P.s, the abolition of all property qualifications for membership, and equal-sized constituencies— have all since been enacted. But it became the focus for all the diverse discontents of the 1830s and attracted the support of every kind of reformer and crank, who used it as cover for their own panaceas : teetotallers and currency reformers, early socialists and Bible evangelists, and those who merely wished to overthrow the government—the physical-forcists. What it could not attract were the business brains and the large funds to organise a successful campaign. For the men who could have supplied these were just those who had won their share in government in 1832 and who were not interested in extending their privilege any further down the social scale.

In fact the Reform Bill achieved the limited objectives of its sponsors very well. It averted immediate revolution and it deprived any future revolutionary movement of the middle-class leadership which would alone make it dangerous. Moreover, it opened the way for the successive governments of Grey and Lord Melbourne to complete the tidying-up process begun by Pitt in 1783, and in the course of it gradually to transform the Whigs into the Liberal party of the 19th century. For by itself Parliamentary Reform was not enough, and something more drastic than the administrative tinkering of the Tories was needed. In the first place Parliamentary Reform made no sense at all if the old, corrupt, muddled, out-of-date borough organisations were left intact. New towns allotted members of Parliament often had no municipal government at all, and in most of the old power had fallen into the hands of a few influential men and racketeers. The Municipal Reform Bill of 1835 established a uniform system of town councils elected by all the ratepayers and empowered to deal with all local services such as sanitation and street paving and lighting.

Still more crying was the need to reform the Poor Law. The Elizabethan system of parish relief had been based on the assumption of a minimum wage fixed in relation to the price of bread so that the poorest could subsist. *Laissez-faire* economics had discredited this interference with the laws of supply and demand, and in the 1790s wages often fell below the actual subsistence level. In 1798, in a well-intentioned effort to remedy this, the Berkshire magistrates meeting at Speenhamland had decided to subsidise labourers' wages in such cases out of the rates. Other counties followed suit, and the result had been wholesale pauperisation. Farmers seized the chance of getting part of their wage bill footed by the ratepayers, and many labourers preferred idleness on outdoor relief to hard work for a very small extra reward; and rates rose from a total of £2 million to over £7 million by 1815.

The core of the problem was of course the exploitation of the honest worker by the idle, and the Poor Law Reform of 1834 tackled it with appalling severity. Only the aged and the sick could be relieved in their own homes. The able-bodied must work or enter one of the new workhouses where life was designedly "as disagreeable as consistent with health", with wives separated from their husbands, a complete absence of minor comforts like tobacco, and with all types, "old and young, infirm and able-bodied, imbeciles and epileptics" herded indiscriminately together. The required result was achieved, but at a cost of great bitterness among the poor which was to persist for more than a century.

The abolition of slavery in 1833 was for the British Empire only a minor reform, though it marked the first step on the road to humanity for the world at large. More immediately important was the first effective Factory Act which, by appointing government inspectors, ensured at last that the conditions laid down for the employment of women and children were properly observed. There were, too, a large number of minor, but not unimportant reforms: the first modest Education Act which allotted £20,000 a year to the voluntary societies supplying free education for factory children; the establishment of prepaid 1d. postage; some equalisation of Church endowments; and improvements in banking practice and of the East India Company's administration. More capital offences were abolished, and even the Game Laws were modified. Meanwhile the last stages of the industrial revolution were completing themselves, and the first 500 miles of railway completed in 1838 were soon to bring prices down all round by providing cheap transport.

In fact a man who lived exclusively in the world of Parliament and City and genteel society could congratulate himself on ten years of spectacular progress which had made England the pleasantest and most progressive country to live in in the world. But the Age of Reason had an infinite capacity for not seeing the realities of poverty and suffering which maintained its outward splendour. There was a brutal inhumanity about much, even, of the reform, and the Factory Acts were remarkable more for what they permitted than for what they forbade. In 1845 the Tory Disraeli could still write in a novel of the "two worlds" of rich and poor which lived side by side in Britain.

Thus Melbourne's government came to an end in an atmosphere not of peace and gratitude but of great Chartist demonstrations, petitions, and riots not merely on behalf of Parliamentary Reform but against all the unremedied hardships which made life still scarcely tolerable for a large minority. In fact the era of reform ushered in a period remembered by the poor as the "hungry forties". True Sir Robert Peel, with a revivified Tory Party which was beginning to call itself Conservative, carried on the work of reform after 1841. There was a Bank Charter Act, and a Mines Act at last prohibited the employment of women and children underground; and another Factory Act cut the working hours of children under thirteen to six and a half a day and of women to twelve. But characteristically, the real work was done by

Peel's free-trade budgets, which transferred part of the burden of taxation from the poor to the rich by Income Tax, and gradually lowered the cost of living to the working man. But there was still left a sufficient volume of discontent to give tremendous impetus to the campaign for repeal of the Corn Laws launched by Cobden and Bright, two of the more enlightened members of the employing class.

From 1840 onwards the Anti-Corn-Law League stole almost all the thunder of the Chartists. Dear bread was a simpler issue for the public than the constitutional refinements of the six points; and it was undeniable that in a bad harvest year the poorest families had to spend two-thirds of their incomes on bread alone. Moreover, business men were directly interested, since cheap bread would damp down the clamour for higher wages and also leave the poor with more to spend on manufactured goods.

It has never been established that the Corn Laws were responsible for the high price of bread. They aimed at keeping wheat at 56s. a quarter, but a shortage of the world's wheat supplies kept the price up without any help; and ten years after the repeal of the laws it was still 53s. 5d. a quarter. But the League's argument that selfish landlords and farmers were starving the poor carried conviction. With large subsidies from the Manchester Chamber of Commerce and the best business brains to run it, the League launched the first great modern propaganda campaign, with mass meetings and millions of pamphlets, and rhymes and posters for the masses who could not read.

Peel had been elected to protect corn, but in 1845 he had been convinced he was wrong. The disastrous Irish potato famine of 1846 completed his conversion, since he believed only cheap corn could save the lives of the teeming Irish peasantry. Actually this argument, too, was fallacious, since the more prosperous districts even of Ireland continued to export wheat and butter throughout the famine. But Peel insisted on abolishing the Corn Laws, splitting his own party irretrievably in the process and ruining his own career, honestly convinced that he had no alternative.

Ineffectual as it was in reducing the price of bread, the Anti-Corn-Law League served the useful political purpose of diverting and canalising much discontent which might otherwise have expressed itself in revolution. And by 1847 the worst of the economic and social crisis really was beginning to pass. The astronomical rise in the figures of industrial production and export trade produced a prosperity so widespread that it was at last reflected in a rise of the real value of wages, even for the poorest classes. A third Factory Act in that year reduced the women's working day to ten hours, and since most mills and many factories could not be run without their labour, the ten-hour day soon became the rule for all. Moreover better organised Trade Unions were discovering better ways of bringing pressure to bear on employers than the futile strikes of the '20s, and were negotiating improvements in conditions beyond the minima laid down by Act of Parliament. The 500 miles of railway of 1838 had become 5,000, and low fares enforced by law had brought the boon of cheap travel to all.

Side by side, moreover, with the economic, social and political alleviations which had gradually eased the situation since 1821, there were spiritual and intellectual forces which had long been at work breaking up that rationalistic detachment which had applied the doctrines of *laissez-faire* so ruthlessly to human lives. The building of John Wesley's first chapel at Bristol in 1739 had heralded an Evangelical revival; and though the Church was slow to wake from her 18th-century torpor, and the Wesleyan movement was allowed to escape into Nonconformity, there was by the end of the century a humanitarian response within the Church itself producing such movements as the Church Missionary Society and Wilberforce's Anti-Slavery Society. Undoubtedly Wesleyanism performed an indirect social service by focusing men's thoughts on a heavenly future instead of the intolerable present on earth; but there was a great deal of more practical application of Christian teaching, much of it by Quakers, in prison reform and in the Charity Schools of the S.P.C.K. which began to give primary education back to the masses.

In the 1820s and '30s the whole spiritual and intellectual climate was changing. The romantic poets, Wordsworth and Coleridge, Shelley and Keats and Byron, had launched the assault on the complacency of the Age of Reason. In response to the Evangelicals there was the great ritualistic revival of the Oxford Movement, reminding the Church sharply of almost forgotten spiritual and pastoral responsibilities, and planting new churches among the industrial masses. There was still enough destitution and misery to justify Disraeli's reproach of the two worlds, but mostly by then it was concentrated among the last workers in the dying industries : Nottinghamshire stockingers and Lancashire handloom weavers for whom there was no remedy but poor relief. The prevailing atmosphere was one of improvement and hopefulness; and Marx and Engels, those two experts on fomenting revolution, concluded after a close analysis that there was not in England in 1848 the quantity or quality of discontent needed for a general rising.

Besides the amelioration of industrial discontent, there were other factors working for political stability. The Reform Bill had given a share of responsibility to almost all those for the time being whose education and standing made them actively desire it. The monarchy, too, had begun to recover from the discredit into which the antics of George III's sons had plunged it with the accession in 1837 of a young and conscientious Queen, and was rapidly becoming a powerful stabilising factor in the national life. Victoria was headstrong and wilful in her early years, and was only saved from several major misjudgements by the tact and wisdom of old Lord Melbourne, whom she adored. But she was a quick learner, and her marriage to her cousin, Prince Albert of Saxe-Coburg, though it was never really popular, certainly imported into the English royal family a tradition of duty and public service which, purged of his slightly over-earnest, Germanic intellectualism, has become one of the most valuable elements in English national life.

Thus, when the revolutionary storm broke over Europe in 1848, and the barricades were across the streets of almost every capital, London experienced only the slightly farcical anti-climax of the Chartist monster petition. Their leaders had hoped to mass a vast gathering on Kennington Common which should march with overwhelming effect on the Houses of Parliament; and twenty years earlier this might have been the prelude to revolution. But there was so little fervour that the troops tactfully arranged round the Common by the aged Commander-in-Chief, the Duke of Wellington, supported by 170,000 volunteer special constables, had no difficulty in preventing the march. The petition, with its boasted five and a half million signatures, was in the end conveyed to Westminster in five hackney carriages, and there many of the signatures were found to be fakes. So the Chartist movement petered out. There was still, of course, shocking inequality and much scandalous poverty, as can be seen from the early novels of Charles Dickens. But enough progress had been made to make men disinclined to risk their gains in the gamble of a violent revolution; and to this happy result Tory reformers, liberalised Whigs, Trade Unionists and philanthropists, Evangelicals and economists had all made their significant contributions.

CHAPTER XIII

The Era of British Supremacy
The Victorian Age
1848 – 1914

FOR a brief space in the latter half of the 19th century Great Britain enjoyed a material prosperity unique in the world's history. To the commercial supremacy inherited from earlier ages there was now added an industrial monopoly which for thirty years put her beyond the reach of foreign competition in almost every branch of production, while the overflow of her teeming population and her huge surplus of capital wealth enabled her to open up vast new areas of the undeveloped world for colonisation, for the exploitation of new sources of raw materials, and as fresh markets for the goods which she alone had to sell. The population rose again, to 35 million. The 5,000 miles of railway of 1848 had further lengthened to 18,000 by 1880. As steam and iron replaced sails and wood on the seas Britain's industrial lead enabled her to supply more than a third of the world's shipping. Production of coal, iron, cotton, and woollen goods increased year by year until, in 1874, the total value of her export trade equalled that of France, Italy, Germany, and the U.S.A. put together. Moreover there was, for the moment, no dangerous unbalancing of the national economy. In 1850 the number of workers employed in agriculture and industry were still roughly equal. Farming and all its dependent rural industries and crafts flourished along with the rest, and there was not yet the dangerous overcrowding which has since made the island's economic existence so precarious.

The Victorians themselves were fond of saying that the middle class was the backbone of the country; and it was, indeed, round an unprecedentedly numerous class of professional and business men that the whole machine of Victorian England revolved. It was they who produced the goods and exploited the new inventions. The younger sons of their huge families went out to explore the new markets and develop the fresh sources of wealth, providing from jute factories in India or African sisal plantations the raw materials for further expansion at home. When the reforms of Dr. Arnold at Rugby opened to them the hitherto aristocratic preserves of the so-called public schools, they thronged eagerly to acquire an education which set more store by character than academic brains. Old grammar schools expanded and adapted themselves to meet this new demand and new schools were founded along Arnold's lines to provide the administrators and pioneers to explore and police and govern and exploit a spreading Empire : men, perhaps, of a grotesquely limited and complacent outlook, profoundly certain of the somewhat crude values acquired as much on the playing fields as in the classroom, but endowed with an integrity and probity and an earnestness of purpose such as few governing classes had been able to show.

At the core of all their activity lay an unshakeable belief in the ordered and, indeed, divinely guided progress of the human race, in which, palpably, Britian had taken the lead. The work of Charles Darwin and the evolutionists seemed to suggest that nature herself had ordained a continuous improvement in the capacities and adaptability of man; so that religious men could see in this rationalist development the purpose of an all-wise creator, while even atheists and agnostics were provided with a dynamic faith driving them to collaborate in this ordered progress of mankind. Political theorists and historians and poets derived the same inspiration from the study of an English past in which freedom had slowly broadened down, as Tennyson put it, "from precedent to precedent", giving the nations a lead to the divinely appointed end : "the Parliament of Man, the Federation of the World". The same fundamental belief inspired every utterance of that greatest of Victorian liberals, Mr. Gladstone, and the history written by Macaulay, the reforming zeal of employers like John Bright, and the work of countless lesser men who sat on the Royal Commissions to modernise the universities, equalise Church revenues, and bring the haphazard, accumulated charities of the past into sensible relation with modern facts.

All this aspect of the Victorian age was perhaps best epitomised by the Great Exhibition which the Prince Consort organised in Hyde Park in 1851. Here, under the somewhat tasteless roof of the Crystal Palace, were gathered examples of all that England had achieved to improve the material lot of the human race. Much of it has deserved the scorn of posterity as inartistic, as did the sentimentalised paintings of Landseer, the imitation baronial country houses, and many of the churches of the Gothic revival. But it was also an age which threw up much immortal literature, such as the poetry of Browning and the novels in which Dickens and Thackeray, in their different ways, castigated and satirised the world in which they lived.

Moreover, though a vastly disproportionate share of the rising wealth and comfort went to the already rich employing classes, there was hardly any section of English society which did not benefit at least indirectly from the rising tide of prosperity. Wages were going up, taxation was very low, and the cheaper goods flooding the markets brought the cost of living steadily down. Led by the progressive Amalgamated Engineering Union, the Trade Unions generally were able to obtain, mainly by negotiation, concessions in hours and wage rates which immensely improved conditions in factories and mines. In this progressive bargaining, in the foundation of the T.U.C. in 1868, and in the development of the Parliamentary Labour Party from 1874 onwards, the working classes were merely conforming to the Victorian utilitarian pattern. The philosopher, Bentham, had taught them the ideal of the greatest happiness of the greatest number, to be achieved by every man seeking his own most enlightened self-interest. This was, indeed, but *laissez-faire* in a new guise; but so long as there was such a plenty to share nearly everybody could benefit from the free operation of laws of supply and demand.

Perhaps most impressive of all the Victorian achievement was the imperialist expansion which by the end of the century had given Britain responsibility for nearly a fifth of the world's land surface and control over more than a third of its raw materials. Thanks largely to the wisdom of Lord Durham in the 1830s, the French and English settlers in Canada had been induced to live peaceably together and had been granted a large measure of self-government. This was the prelude to a century of expansion westwards, until the federated provinces of the Dominion of Canada stretched to the Pacific. Vastly different beginnings in the convict settlements of Australia produced in due course another great self-governing Commonwealth, less populous than Canada but enriched by the best sheep-grazing in the world. The two great neighbouring islands which made up New Zealand were also settled, more 'systematically', by the initiative of Gibbon Wakefield, with selected colonisers who made from the start a well-balanced community.

The original Maori inhabitants of New Zealand, unlike most Canadian Indians and the Blackfellows of Australia, were able eventually to take full advantage of the civilisation of their new neighbours and to aspire to a full and equal share in the government of their Dominion. It remained, nevertheless in Canada and Australia, essentially a transplantation of British people, institutions, and ideas overseas, and these were the most successful aspect of the 19th century British imperialism. In the various provinces which were later, in 1909, to join up as the Union of South Africa, British domination was never so complete. The Dutch were first in the field and preponderant in the white population; and there was no agreed policy as to the rights of native communities. Similarly elsewhere, in Africa, in India and Burma, Malaya, and even in the older colonies of the West Indies, British penetration was too superficial to constitute a real colonisation. A long series of colonial, frontier, and tribal campaigns in every quarter of the globe brought British sovereignty, peace, law, order, and protection, and generally a greatly increased prosperity. But the soldiers and administrators, traders and industrialists retired in the end with their fortunes or their pensions to their native country.

In the prosperous Victorian heyday the novel benefits of civilised government kept these native populations on the whole contented enough, and their produce went to swell the already vast British wealth and power. But the great mutiny of the East India Company's native troops in 1875, when all but a few murdered their British officers and attempted, with dissident native Princes, to expel the British, was a warning of the dangers of the system. The heroism of a few loyal garrisons and of a handful of British regiments saved all for the time being. The government took over from the Company all political responsibility; and in 1877 the Conservative Prime Minister, Disraeli, persuaded Queen Victoria to assume the title of Empress of India. For a brief space the diverse races, religions, and cultures of India were thus united under a single rule, and one which gave them better government than ever before. The problem of the proper relationship between an increasingly educated and self-conscious native population and an alien ruling caste was, however, shelved, to become the most intractable of Britain's difficulties in the following century.

Meanwhile preoccupation with her internal progress and overseas expansion kept Britain somewhat aloof from European politics. The weight of her influence was thrown always on the side of peace, which she needed for trade, especially by the greatest of her Foreign Secretaries, Lord Palmerston; and when the balance of power broke down she kept out of the great wars of the middle of the century out of which there emerged the new European powers of the German Empire and the Kingdom of Italy. She was obliged to intervene when there was danger of France again annexing Belgium in 1830, and Palmerston eventually achieved what looked like a permanent solution of this problem by getting a new Kingdom of Belgium set up whose perpetual neutrality was guaranteed by all the great powers. Only in 1854 did the threat of another great power, this time Russia, to acquire a land route to India actually force her into a major war.

Skilful diplomacy might have prevented the Crimean War; but a number of trivial incidents and disputes were allowed to grow into a serious attempt by Russia to smash the decaying Turkish Empire and seize Constantinople. This, traditionally, Britain felt bound to oppose, not so much because it would give the Russian Black Sea fleet access to the Mediterranean through the Dardanelles, as for fear that Russian armies in Asia Minor might threaten the peace of India and Africa. Palmerston had met this threat already once, in the 1830s, and by 'bounce and bluff' had prevented either France or Russia getting a foothold in Syria and Egypt. In 1854 Aberdeen's government felt obliged to join the French in rescuing Turkey, and a singularly pointless campaign was fought in the Crimean Peninsular to capture and destroy the great Russian naval base at Sebastopol. In spite of indifferent generalship, out-of-date tactics and weapons, and an administrative incompetence which has become legendary, the fortress was destroyed; and the fumbling 'soldiers' battles' of the Alma, Balaclava and Inkerman added the fame of the Heavy and Light Brigade charges and the 'Thin Red Line' to British military history. But the sufferings and losses of the troops, in tropical kit and without tents in face of a Russian winter, and with no proper medical equipment, were appalling; and the only ultimate benefit was the improved standard of nursing service forced on the authorities by Florence Nightingale and her heroic band of helpers in the base hospital at Scutari.

The Congress of Paris in 1856 succeeded in the main object of halting the Russian advance, but the Eastern Question remained a major object of British preoccupation down to the end of the century. When the cutting of the Suez Canal immensely shortened the sea route to India, Disraeli thought it prudent to secure financial control of it; and to secure that, in turn, successive British governments were forced to establish a Protectorate over Egypt and the Sudan, so rousing the jealous hostility of

France. Other large African acquisitions—the combined fruit of Dr. Livingstone's explorations and the expansionist ambitions of Cecil Rhodes—roused the even greater jealousy of the new Germany, stridently claiming a "place in the sun" for herself; and by the end of the century Britain was forced back into the theatre of European politics by the mere fact that isolation combined with the tremendous growth of her power and wealth had provoked the hostility of all her neighbours.

By then, as the historian can now see, the climax of Victorian greatness was past. In the first place cheap oceanic steam transport after 1860 began to flood the English market with American and Canadian corn and ruined the unprotected arable farming industry. Before long refrigeration brought cheap meat as well from the Argentine, Australia, and New Zealand and completed the irretrievable destruction of English agriculture. With it went the whole traditional way of life, the age-old crafts and skills and industries so wistfully commemorated in the Wessex novels of Thomas Hardy. Such labourers as were not forced to drift into the towns in search of other employment were left barely subsisting on wages of 10s. a week, and Britain became wholly and dangerously dependent on imported food. The labour was absorbed in the towns and the nation continued to get richer, though the national life, increasingly urbanised and congested, was immeasurably impoverished.

The effect of this became all the more serious when, from 1870 onwards, the basic export industries began to face growing foreign competition. Germany and the U.S.A. first, and then in due course France and Italy, Japan, the great overseas Dominions, and even India, began the process of industrial revolution, coming into the market with untapped sources of iron and coal when the best of Britain's were already worked out, and drawing on unlimited supplies of labour accustomed to lower wages and longer hours than the English. From 1890 onwards English coal-mining was fighting a losing battle and standards were beginning to decline. The textile industries held their own for a little by replacing lost European markets in Africa and the Far East; but this was a precarious survival, doomed as soon as it was challenged by Japanese and Indian cotton mills.

The process of decline was slow. The established position and experience of British manufacturers and the high quality of their finished products long enabled them, as it still does, just to hold their own; and the whole danger was masked by the still rising profits of shipping and banking, and of the vast accumulated 'invisible exports' of foreign investment. The national income still rose year by year, and in 1914 the Empire's trade was valued at the staggering total of £1,100 million. But the real value of wages was declining and with it standards of housing and feeding. Slum clearance was checked by the need to provide for fresh increases of population, while the rejection of two out of every three army recruits as physically unfit showed under-nourishment dangerously widespread. Moreover, there was an irreducible total of unemployment which was neither seasonal nor transitional but permanent, and it rose steadily every year.

Thus when the Queen's death brought the Victorian age to an end in 1902 the fabric of British prosperity and power was already very brittle. New wealth was more and more concentrated in the hands of the prosperous few, and it depended too much on easily repudiated foreign investments and a commerce too easily excluded by a world which was to be dominated for the next half-century, in peace as in war, by an hysterical nationalism. It is small wonder that to a thinking few the rich, self-indulgent, pleasure-seeking world of King Edward VII seemed to be dancing its waltzes and its new-fangled ragtime on the brink of a catastrophe.

The South African War really marked the end of the Victorian calm. The basic opposition between the Dutch Boer farmers, who had twice migrated—from Cape Colony and Natal—to preserve their independence, and the followers of Rhodes who dreamt of a self-governing dominion of South Africa was made irreconcilable by the hesitations of government policy at home. It was not only greed for the newly discovered gold and diamonds of the

Transvaal which drove the British forward. The Boers were intolerant and intolerable neighbours, brutal in their handling of all native affairs, anxious to exclude all foreigners from their territories, though ready enough to depend on British help against Kaffirs or Zulus when in trouble. Consistent firmness might have amended this; but British vacillation encouraged the Boer President, Kruger, to an unco-operative defiance, and government incompetence then contrived that there were only 14,000 troops available against 60,000 Boers when war finally broke out in 1899.

British complacency consequently suffered two severe shocks. The outnumbered British went forward, scarlet-coated and in close order, as easy targets for Boers who were born hunters and marksmen, and in one 'black week' lost three battles. For a time it even seemed impossible to relieve the besieged garrisons of Ladysmith, Mafeking, and Kimberley. At the same time a world-wide chorus of denunciation of British aggression and of rejoicing at Boer successes woke the nation up to its dangerous isolation and the jealous hostility of rivals who had been outstripped. Once a serious effort was made, of course, Lord Roberts and Lord Kitchener had little difficulty in winning the war, though it was June 1902 before the last guerrilla commandos were rounded up and peace was made on wisely generous terms. The Republics were annexed, but were promised early self-government and given £3 million for reconstruction; and so rapid was the pacification thanks largely to a brilliant team of young administrators led by Lord Milner, that in 1909 Rhodes' self-governing Union of South Africa came into being, and its first Prime Minister was the Boer General Botha.

The problem of British isolation was more troublesome. Germany was already building a fleet which could only be intended to challenge British naval supremacy, unquestioned since Trafalgar, and so enable her to extend the slender foothold she had won in Africa. Russia, the ancient enemy, had expanded eastwards so rapidly that she now threatened India's northern passes as well as Asia Minor. Italian ambitions, as well as French, were frustrated by British control of the Nile Valley; and no tie of blood or language could make the Americans quite forget their deep-rooted suspicion of British imperialism. Moreover, the Triple Alliance of Germany, Austria, and Italy represented such a military threat to the rest of the world that France and Russia had drawn together in turn into a Dual Alliance, and friendship with one group must mean the enmity of the other. In the end a deep mistrust of Prussian militarism and of the stupid, aggressive utterances of the German Emperor, Kaiser William II, coupled with the German refusal to abandon naval competition, turned the scales in favour of France. The Triple Entente which replaced the Dual Alliance did not in theory commit England to fight. But it was increasingly clear to Englishmen that, if they did not assist France and Russia, they would have to face single-handed a Germany drunk with dreams of world power.

At home, too, the placid certainties of Victorianism disintegrated so fast that by 1914 the country almost seemed to be on the verge of revolution. Against a background of prosperity and low taxation the political battles of Gladstone and Disraeli had been almost a game, watched with the same quality of enthusiasm as a century at Lord's by W. G. Grace. The election of a Liberal government in 1906, supported by over fifty Labour members, and pledged to reforms which heralded the beginnings of Socialism, changed the whole tone. The fiery Welsh Chancellor of the Exchequer, David Lloyd George, really dominated the government led by Asquith; and he was determined to make the rich pay in super-tax and death duties for Old Age Pensions, a rudimentary health service, unemployment insurance, and an expanded free education service. The enraged Conservatives in the House of Lords defied all custom and precedent by throwing out his budget in 1909, and so provoked a major political crisis. The country was torn by a bitter fight over the Parliament Act, which deprived the Lords of their absolute veto; and it was not until the new King, George V, who succeeded in 1910, had threatened to swamp the Conservative majority by creating some 500 Liberal peers that the Bill went through.

As a background to this there was widespread labour unrest which forced the government at one stage to send troops into the South Wales coalfields. Women who called themselves Suffragettes added to the confusion by clamouring for the vote and supporting their clamour by every kind of outrage : bombs in pillar boxes, assaults on public men, arson, and the smashing of works of art; and finally a crisis in Ireland brought the country, as George V remarked, to the verge of civil war.

The Irish crisis arose directly out of the fact that the Liberals could not force the Parliament Act through the Commons without the seventy votes of the Irish nationalists and had to promise in return Home Rule for Ireland. Encouraged by the Conservatives, the Protestant Unionists of Northern Ireland rejected any form of union with the Catholic south, and by 1914 they were importing rifles and machine-guns and drilling thousands of volunteers. The Nationalists began counter-measures, and it became clear that the government could not count on the loyalty of its officers if it attempted to coerce Ulster.

It is hard to see how an Irish civil war could have been avoided, had not an Austrian Archduke suddenly been murdered by a Serb nationalist at Sarajevo. None of the powers really wanted a general war. But the Austrians tried to seize the opportunity of eliminating Serbia without clearly realising that the Russians would certainly come to the aid of their Slav cousins; and Germany rather carelessly pledged support to Austria in the same mistaken belief. As all the powers, including France, began to arm, Great Britain at last had to face the real meaning of the half-commitments made to France in the Triple Entente. At the critical moment English policy wavered, Conservatives sharing the view of Grey, the Foreign Secretary, that France must be supported at all costs, Liberals being reluctant to fight for Russian Balkan quarrels. But the German announcement of their intention to invade Belgium in defiance of international guarantees settled the matter.

A united nation stood behind the declaration of war on 4th August; for the English were convinced that there was a bully loose in the world once again, and even the Irish Nationalists pledged their support in dealing with the matter.

CHAPTER XIV

The First Great Struggle for Freedom and its Aftermath
1914–1939

WHATEVER the diplomatic arguments for or against intervention, basically the situation was the same in 1914 as under Pitt. Once again England had ranged herself against 'armed opinion', this time in the shape of Prussian militarism, whose dreams of world power and disregard for international law represented the same sort of threat as had Philip II, Louis XIV, and Napoleon. Lloyd George summed up the feeling of his contemporaries when he said they fought "to make the world safe for democracy". It was a war, moreover, which could only be won by Pitt's basic method : a Continental coalition to contain the enemy in Europe until naval blockade sapped his strength and broke his will.

There was, however, one important difference from the Napoleonic situation. 1914 embodied Clausewitz's Prussian conception of whole nations, rather than professional armies, mobilised for war, and defeat was likely to be total and irremediable. There would be no dogged re-forming of coalitions if the first was allowed to collapse, and at all costs France had to be kept in the war. The powerful German right hook through Belgium was intended to swing the French armies back round Paris on to their own fortified Verdun–Belfort frontier line and annihilate them before their ponderous Russian allies got going. The small, highly efficient British Expeditionary Force could not therefore be used in its most effective rôle as an amphibious striking force on the enemy's left flank, but had to be flung in at once on the left of the French line and engulfed in the great battle of the Marne. In the costly, brilliantly conducted retreat from Mons, and in the counter-thrust which halted the Germans north of Paris it played its part nobly. But by the end of September the British were committed to holding the north-western end of a line which stretched from the North Sea to Switzerland, entrenched behind barbed wire in a war of attrition which put unprecedented strains on their resources. The Russians blundered forward to disaster at Tannenberg and their front, too, settled down into a continuous line. The war thus became a siege of the central powers of Germany, Austria, Turkey, and Bulgaria, complete when Italy joined against her old allies in 1915.

For four years both sides strove in vain to break the deadlock imposed by barbed wire and the machine-guns which mowed down the attacking infantry in spite of the pulverising artillery barrages which preceded every assault. To save the heavily outnumbered French, Britain and her Empire had to mobilise and train armies on a scale never before imagined. Lord Kitchener, now War Minister, raised a volunteer army of two million men, flung in in 1915 to replace the regular and territorial divisions battered to pieces round Ypres. But until Lloyd George took over a new Ministry of Munitions there were not enough heavy guns or high-explosive shells to give the great attacks at Loos and on the Somme any real chance of success; and these new armies, too, the flower of young English manhood, were butchered in costly, useless fighting which the generals themselves could only justify by the need to relieve hard-pressed allies. After 1916 the nation overcame its dislike of compulsory military service, and more millions of conscripts went in, to become casualties in their turn. Loos alone cost the British 60,000 men; the Somme 60,000 on the first day, and 400,000 casualties in all. By 1918 Sir Douglas Haig, who had taken over command from Sir John French, had to be warned that his summer attack had to be the last, since there were no more able-bodied men to be conscripted.

Inevitably both sides sought feverishly for some means of avoiding these suicidal frontal attacks, and each in fact developed in turn a weapon which, properly used, might have achieved a decisive breakthrough. But the German poison gas, which added another horror to war, was so unexpectedly successful that no reserves were at hand to exploit the success; and the British invention of the tank was similarly wasted by the failure of conservative-minded generals to seize on its possibilities in time. There was also the possibility for Britain at least, of turning the trench lines by finding a back door into the Central European citadel. The genius of Winston Churchill, First Lord of the Admiralty, suggested one such attempt at Gallipoli in 1915. Had it been even reasonably handled by the higher command, that attack might have knocked Turkey out of the war and opened up a supply line to keep Russia in it. But by careless security, incompetent loading of supplies, and administrative delay, speed and surprise were forfeited, and the joint assault by navy and army just failed to carry the Straits of the Dardanelles at the first rush. After four months of heroic fighting, particularly by the Australian and New Zealand Corps, the whole attempt had to be abandoned; and subsequent attempts at Salonika on the Aegean, and in Palestine, were too late to be decisive, though Allenby's capture of Jerusalem, brilliantly assisted by Colonel Lawrence and the Arabs, did knock Turkey out just before the collapse of her allies.

For the Germans the obvious short cut to victory was at sea. Sir John Jellicoe, commanding the British Grand Fleet, was, in Churchill's graphic phrase, the one man who could "lose the war in an afternoon". The German High Seas Fleet was not strong enough to risk a major engagement until it had worn down Jellicoe's strength by a series of partial successes. But the bombardment of English east-coast resorts never quite succeeded in tempting a part of the Grand Fleet into sacrificing itself in a mine or submarine trap, or in a battle with superior German forces. One such attempt in 1916 did, however, bring about at Jutland the meeting of the two great fleets at full strength of which every English seaman dreamed. There the Germans had rather the better of the early tactical exchanges; bad light and nightfall deprived Jellicoe of an annihilating victory at the moment when he had established a decisive superiority; and a series of unlucky accidents allowed the Germans to slip back into safety during the night.

More serious, and more nearly successful, was the German attempt to knock England out of the war by a counter-blockade enforced by submarines which sank without warning any merchant ship, allied or neutral, since all must be indirectly serving Germany's enemies. This flagrant defiance of international law was abandoned when the sinking of the Cunard liner, *Lusitania*, with the loss of 1,200 civilian lives all but brought the U.S.A. into the war. After Jutland it was ruthlessly renewed by large numbers of U-boats, and the U.S. declaration of war duly followed. But American armies had to be raised and trained, and meanwhile the loss of British shipping rose from 300,000 tons a month in 1916 to 900,000 tons in April of 1917. England was within six weeks of starvation long before American divisions could begin to turn the tide of battle in France, and a system of protected convoys and improved techniques of submarine destruction saved her only just in time.

The crisis of the war for the Allies lasted from the spring of 1917 until April 1918. Russia collapsed under the strain and disintegrated in revolution. Rumania was overrun. The great German-Austrian victory at Caporetto in October all but destroyed the Italian army. American help was still far off, the French troops were exhausted, and Britain was fighting off the threat of starvation. In that year England abandoned the last vestiges of the comfort-loving conventions of the Victorian age and set herself to learn something of the methods of total war. Conscription had already been accepted, and already the party system had been abandoned : it was a Coalition government directed by Lloyd George which rallied the country to its last dogged effort. Food was tightly rationed. The Defence of the Realm Act abolished Habeas Corpus. Trade Unions gave up cherished rights, hours and standards, permitting the dilution of skilled labour and the replacement of men by women in factories, and abandoned the right to strike. After a century of liberalism and

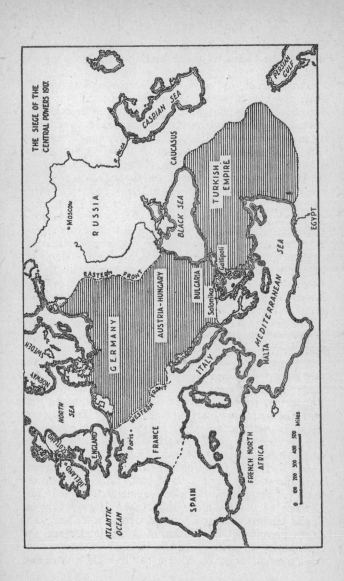

THE SIEGE OF THE
CENTRAL POWERS 1917

ATLANTIC
OCEAN

NORTH
SEA

NORWAY

SWEDEN

SCOTLAND

IRELAND

ENGLAND

Paris

FRANCE

SPAIN

FRENCH NORTH
AFRICA

GERMANY

AUSTRIA-HUNGARY

ITALY

WESTERN FRONT

EASTERN FRONT

RUSSIA

Moscow

CASPIAN SEA

BLACK SEA

CAUCASUS

BULGARIA

Salonika

Gallipoli

TURKISH
EMPIRE

MEDITERRANEAN
SEA

MALTA

EGYPT

PERSIAN
GULF

100 200 300 400 500 Miles

laissez-faire these were not easy sacrifices, and inexperience produced a good deal of muddle and grumbling. But morale held, as it had in Pitt's blackest years; and by the spring of 1918, with two million Americans beginning to arrive on the French battlefields, victory was in sight.

The German leaders could see this too. Their civilian morale was wearing thin under the prolonged blockade; their armies were exhausted and there was a dangerous lack of equipment; and it would be at least a year before Rumanian oil and corn from the Ukraine could relieve their most dangerous shortages. Ludendorff, the brain behind all the later German strategy, therefore risked all on a final military victory in France. In March 1918 he used the divisions set free from the Russian front to create an overwhelming numerical superiority before the Americans turned the scale; and by infiltration tactics which made nonsense of all previous military thinking on both sides he all but split the British armies from the French in a series of brilliant attacks. Outnumbered by more than two to one, the British 4th and 5th Armies only just held together and saved the key base at Amiens. Haig, an unimaginative general but a great leader, threw his last reserve in and called on his troops to fight it out "with their backs to the wall." They responded nobly, and the French by similar exertions held the subsidiary German attacks on the Marne. In July Haig flung his exhausted troops back on to the attack, and a converging Franco-American thrust from the south-west rolled the Germans back across the ground they had held for four years until, on 11th November when Ludendorff surrendered unconditionally to gain an Armistice, the British stood again in front of Mons.

So once more Britain faced the consequences of a total war to defeat foreign despotism. But this time there was to be no quick recovery as there had been after 1815. It was the U.S.A. who now had the technical advantages, the untapped natural resources, and the reserves of manpower to supply the needs of a battered world. Absorbed in a life-and-death struggle and virtually isolated by blockade, Britain had lost valuable markets, some of them for good, to America, Japan, and India. Few of her allies were able to repay what she had unstintedly lent them, while she herself was to make a noble effort to pay off a vast debt to the U.S.A. Direct taxation was seven times what it had been in 1914 and prices had doubled. War had shattered much of the world's banking and credit system centred on London, and the New York bankers were to indulge in dangerous, ultimately fatal, speculative policies.

With her international position permanently impaired, Britain had to face, as in 1815, accumulated domestic problems. Postponement of Home Rule at the outbreak of war had provoked the Easter Rebellion of 1916 in Ireland out of which had grown, in effect, a civil war. This Lloyd George wisely liquidated by giving three-quarters of Ireland self-government in 1921. But it needed another civil war to establish the Irish Free State, and even that, in due course, repudiated allegiance to the English Crown and became the Republic of Eire; while the retention of Ulster created the issue of Partition which has remained a running sore and has come to a grievous head in 1973.

Another immediate necessity was political reform. Both Disraeli and Gladstone had widened the franchise of 1832 to give the vote to skilled artisans. Now it seemed impossible to deny the vote to all, when all had been required to risk their lives, and manhood suffrage was introduced immediately after the Armistice, along with the overdue grant of votes to women over thirty. In 1928 even that restriction disappeared, and universal suffrage—an end in no way visualised by the reformers of 1832—was at last achieved. Fisher's Education Act raised the school-leaving age to fourteen and abolished the last vestiges of child labour, while some provision was made for the further education of all to the age of eighteen. At the same time India was rewarded for the one and a quarter million she had sent to fight by an accelerated programme of self-government, the move was begun towards complete independence of the Dominions, and the Egyptian Protectorate was ended, only a small guard being left on the Suez Canal.

It was not so easy to provide the "homes fit for heroes" promised by Lloyd George, and many of them found the vote a poor compensation for the social and industrial conditions of the next twenty years. Remarkable strides in social improvement were in fact made. By 1929 real wages had risen by an average of eight per cent and the working day was shorter than in the U.S.A. There were more insured workers than ever before, improved pensions for old men and widows, steadily better education and hospital services, and an all-too-small 'dole' for those out of work. But all this, and the recovery of banking and commerce and the recovery of the gold standard, was bought at the expense of what had once been the most prosperous basic industries. Artificially expanded by war demands, they were hardest hit by the post-war slump, and the irreducible minimum of a million unemployed was mostly concentrated in a few black areas : on the Tyneside and in South Wales coalfields, and among the mills of South Lancashire. Many employers, hard hit since before the war, lacked capital to modernise plant, and a century of competition-free activity had left them dangerously inflexible and unadventurous.

The crisis came in 1926 with a strike by the miners whose wages and conditions were worse than in 1914, and it brought all the workers in Britain out in a sympathetic General Strike which many expected to culminate in revolution. Fortunately the good sense acquired in a thousand years of varied self-government prevailed. Improvised volunteer organisations preserved all the essential services, but it was not that nor the army and police that broke the strike. It ended of itself as men realised that such methods ruined all and benefited none, and somehow infringed the unwritten rules by which Englishmen judge 'fairness'. But the real grievances of the miners were not fair either, and this widespread feeling produced Labour for the first time as the strongest party in the House of Commons of 1929.

The political situation immediately after the war had been confused. Lloyd George had tried to carry on with his Coalition government after winning the so-called 'khaki' election to the cry of "Hang the Kaiser". But the nervous energy which had saved England in war spent itself in intrigues and wrangles which culminated in a Conservative rebellion, a great Liberal defeat, and a long period of government by Stanley Baldwin. In truth Liberalism was a dying force. Its principles, rooted in *laissez-faire* and the 19th-century individualism, made little sense in the hotly competitive, nationalist, and protectionist post-war world. After 1923 the fight was between Conservatives and Socialists, and the Liberals only achieved occasional importance by holding the balance.

Ramsay MacDonald and his able Chancellor of the Exchequer, Philip Snowden, did not get a fair chance to try out socialist theories in 1929. Not only did they depend on Liberal votes for a majority. A multitude of circumstances combined at that moment to produce a world-wide slump of unprecedented magnitude. The attempt to make Germany pay for the damage she had inflicted, conservative deflationary monetary policies, the brilliant recovery of German heavy industry, and a wild, over-confident boom both in production and share values in the U.S.A.—all these contributed to a sudden glut of the world's markets and a Wall Street crash reminiscent of South Sea Bubble days.

The ruin of most of the world's primary producers left Britain's customers without purchasing power, and Britain in turn without the taxable resources to finance socialist experiments. Industry after industry partially closed down and unemployment rose to over three million; and in 1932 England had to go off gold again. The crisis produced another Coalition, a National Government, first under Ramsay MacDonald and then Baldwin, which slowly weathered the storm. The hardest-hit industries were saved by high protective tariffs; agriculture by tariffs, quotas, and subsidies. Imperial preference agreements with the Dominions, negotiated in a great conference at Ottawa in 1932, did something to free Britain from dependence on world conditions she could not control; and sound, conservative finance gradually restored British credit. Recovery was slow and partial, and there remained a million unemployed. But there was promise of better things when all other considerations were suddenly over-shadowed by a renewed threat of war.

The Allies of 1918 had fought "a war to end war", but they differed sadly and fatally in their proposals for perpetual peace. President Wilson of the United States incorporated into the Treaty of Versailles—the final peace of 1919—arrangements for establishing a League of Nations at Geneva, where the method of argument and agreement and collective security was to be substituted for the old diplomacy based on the threat of armed force. Unfortunately, however, none of the great powers made any intelligent use of it. A great revulsion of American feeling against foreign commitments resulted in the repudiation of Wilson by his own countrymen, and the U.S.A. never joined. Russia, preoccupied with her own revolutionary experiment, held aloof until 1934. Germany was treated as an outcast and only admitted in 1926. For French statesmen the only sure way to peace was to break up the Austrian Empire into its component nationalities, to keep Germany permanently disarmed, and France herself strong. The Italians emerged from a period of political and economic chaos with a Fascist government under Mussolini which encouraged the military virtues and nursed imperialistic dreams in the Mediterranean incompatible with League ideals; and the British, exhausted and peace-loving, rather easily convinced themselves that the job was done once Germany was disarmed, and that the democracies would now settle down in amity together. French fears were belittled. Everything was to be left to the League; and Britain cut her armaments down far below the limit of safety and obstinately kept them so.

The result was the worst of all the available worlds. French hostility and suspicion nourished German grievances, prevented all treaty revision, and used the League merely to keep Germany down. The new German Republic could not suppress powerful elements which refused to accept defeat and worked ceaselessly for revenge; and Britain, wilfully blind to German rearmament and the evasion of the Versailles disarmament clauses, thwarted French efforts to make Germany pay for her misdeeds.

Meanwhile the nationalist bickerings and the economic insufficiency of the new small nations in Europe produced ceaseless unrest and quarrels; and the great depression of 1929-32, which hit Germany particularly hard, gave a golden opportunity to unscrupulous politicians who laid the blame for everything on foreign powers, and suggested rearmament and war as the only solution.

Between 1930 and 1939 Britain was offered chance after chance of avoiding ultimate calamity at relatively small cost. The mistaken idealism of some and the Micawberish selfishness and laziness of many more prevented her from taking them. The Japanese invaded Manchuria in defiance of the League, and Britain refused to collaborate in any armed intervention to stop them. Once it became clear that a League condemnation was an empty form, and that Britain would not back its decisions with force, collective security ceased to exist. Mussolini followed the Japanese example by conquering Abyssinia. Adolf Hitler destroyed the German Republic by inflaming and exploiting the worst of nationalist passions, and, in a series of brilliant coups each of which gauged to a nicety French and English reluctance to meet force with force, reoccupied the demilitarised Rhineland in 1935, invaded and annexed Austria in 1937, and by 1938 had made himself so formidable, particularly in the air, that the Western powers left Czecho-Slovakia at his mercy, and so lost the last chance of combining an alliance which might have stopped the Germans overrunning Europe.

No class or party in England, and very few individuals, can be held blameless for this sorry story. The nation as a whole was hysterically bent on avoiding the discomfort and expense of rearming to meet the threat, and utterly unwilling to face the facts. A few politicians had the courage to tell the unpopular truth, among them notably Winston Churchill and Anthony Eden, who resigned his Foreign Secretaryship when the government refused to risk war over Abyssinia. The rest preferred not to lose votes by voicing unpalatable facts, and the nation was glad enough to be deceived. Frenzied and rejoicing crowds greeted Neville Chamberlain, Baldwin's successor, when he returned from Munich in 1938 with a handful of Hitler's worthless paper promises in exchange for disarming the Czechs. Only that winter when the promises had been broken did the government and nation settle grimly down to create the air force, fleet, and army which would once again be needed to save civilisation; and by then it was almost too late.

In spite of all the obvious shortcomings of the generation which, between the two wars, had been too idle, selfish and pleasure-loving to consolidate the peace and security so hardly won in 1918, it was a much more closely united England which faced Hitler's threat to civilisation in 1939 than the nation divided against itself of 1914. The real weaknesses were all on the surface; shortages of aircraft and tanks and trained manpower, and a factory programme which would take more than two years to get into full production. These might well have proved fatal, but with time and luck could be remedied. A foreigner, familiar only with the headlines of English news, might well also have expected a wavering of morale such as was to prove fatal to France. The General Strike; the Statute of Westminster in 1931 which apparently dissipated the Empire by giving the Dominions complete independence; the loosening of ties with India as a result of Gandhi's Home Rule campaign; the blow to the monarchy's prestige when in 1936 the new King, Edward VIII, universally popular as Prince of Wales, found that the nation would not accept the woman of his choice as Queen—all these had helped to strengthen the German belief in the decadence of Western democracy.

In fact these were all deceptive. The salutary shock of the strike and the slump had forced on all classes and creeds a far more sympathetic and intelligent understanding of social and industrial relations. Nowhere had the rich made larger sacrifices in taxation to alleviate the most crying evils, the Conservatives had accepted what was, in effect, a programme of slowed-up socialism by a progressive state supervision of housing and welfare and industrial relations. Similarly the Labour Party, sprung originally from Marxist theories of class war, had accepted a more gradual, non-revolutionary approach to its ideals, working through existing institutions and adapting rather than destroying. Dominion independence had only removed grievances, and the economic and sentimental ties of Empire remained stronger than ever. The sober, conscientious, unassuming way in which Edward VIII's brother, George VI, and his Queen, Elizabeth, shouldered the burden of the Crown after the tragedy left monarchy in England stronger, not weaker, and a stable rallying-point for all classes and creeds. The real clue to English feeling was to be found not in the hysterical relief which greeted Chamberlain after Munich, but the deep, universal resentment and shame when the Czechs were treacherously overrun three months later. A solid national opinion endorsed the guarantee immediately given to Poland, who was Hitler's next designated victim, and did not waver even when Russia betrayed the West by signing a pact of non-aggression with Germany in August of 1939. A month later Hitler invaded Poland and England found herself again at war.

CHAPTER XV

The Second Great Struggle for Freedom and its Consequences
1939 – 1973

IN that first winter of what came to be called the Phoney War there was nothing Britain could do to save Poland from the overwhelming German superiority in numbers, equipment, and aircraft. France, obsessed with the memory of the blood-bath of Verdun, would take no risk; and in 1940 both nations paid in full for the self-indulgent follies of the inter-war years. When Hitler turned his forces west in the spring nothing could be done to save Denmark and Holland. The attempts to help Norway revealed only the impotence of sea-power faced, in coastal waters, with overwhelming air superiority and the fact that English military leaders had learnt nothing from the blunders of Gallipoli. A more serious attempt to defend Belgium suffered disaster when the French line was pierced at Sedan. The British were lucky to rescue most of their troops, though none of their equipment, from the Dunkirk beaches; and France, after a feeble further resistance, ignominiously capitulated.

So, as so often before, a great war opened for Britain with a series of disasters; and, once again, the nation showed its real quality. Though the Dominions supported her magnificently and American material aid was made freely available, the brunt fell inevitably on Britain herself; and the Battle of Britain in September, 1940, was the battle of the civilised world. With an army and Home Guard ludicrously under-equipped and a Navy woefully short of ships, she outfaced the greatest of all her crises. Three things saw her through: the matchless courage and endurance of a handful of young fighter pilots; the imperturbable and inspiring leadership of Churchill, called in at last to deal with disasters he, almost alone, had consistently prophesied; and the indomitable cheerfulness and will to resist of the humblest people who continued to live and work among the rubble of their homes and factories. By the spring of 1941 it was clear that the morale of the German air force was broken, and not that of the British people; and Hitler, like Napoleon and Philip II of Spain, faced the problem of the inaccessibility of an island power which he could not defeat in the air or at sea.

As in the deadlock of 1806, there was no obvious way in which either side could defeat the other. But, like Napoleon, Hitler could not let his New Order in Europe, proclaimed to last for a thousand years, crumble under an iron blockade. Again like Napoleon, he tried to break out through Egypt, using Italian North Africa as his springboard. But the heroism of the people and garrison of Malta under incessant air attack enabled the Navy to keep a Mediterranean supply route open. So General Wavell, with laughably inadequate forces, fought off the Italian army and, in 1942, Montgomery won decisively against both Germans and Italians at Alamein, not only saving Egypt, but paving the way for the conquest of all North Africa. At the same time, having overcome the heroic resistance of Jugo-Slavia and Greece, Hitler dared not exploit this alternative route east with a potentially hostile Russia on his flank. So he set himself to capture Moscow, and the parallel with Napoleon was complete.

But by then the war had ceased to be European and had become global. In December, 1941, the Japanese had launched surprise attacks on the American fleet in Pearl Harbour and on the British and Dutch possessions in the Far East. For a time this attack carried all before it. Burma and Malaya were overrun and the great base at Singapore, reinforced too late, was forced to surrender. In the end the Japanese advance was halted on the northeastern frontier of India, in the Indian Ocean, on the north coast of Australia and along the eastern fringe of the Pacific islands; and in due course the Japanese were driven back. But their irruption into areas where British, Dutch, and French rule had preserved peace for more than a century released forces of nationalism and communism which made any restoration of the old state of affairs unthinkable. Two warning atomic bombs in the summer of 1945 forced the final surrender of Japan, only to leave the West with an even more difficult enemy in Communist China and with insoluble problems in the disintegrated colonial territories, where inexperienced politicians were left to wrestle with problems of over-population and shortage of capital amidst passions and prejudices easily aroused and impossible to control.

Meanwhile the massive help available from America and the fact that Hitler's forces were pinned down before the Russian defences of Moscow and the oilfields of the Caucasus made it possible to storm his 'fortress of Europe' from the west. One great combined operation freed the French provinces in North Africa, linked up with Montgomery's 8th Army, overran Sicily, and pushed on into what Churchill called the "soft under-belly" of the Axis powers in Italy. More immediately decisive, however, was the assault on the heavily defended Normandy coast by the Anglo-American forces in June, 1944. By then the Russians had driven the German armies back to their own frontiers, and two years of pulverising air attack by the combined air forces of Britain and America had gone far to paralyse German communications and slow up their industrial production. This made it possible, after heavy fighting, to make good the Normandy bridgehead. The Americans broke out of Avranches in a great sweep which freed all France, while Montgomery caught and destroyed the German army of the west at Falaise.

Hitler had encouraged the German people to fight to the bitter end with promises of new Victory weapons which would suddenly turn the scale; and in fact two of them—V1 and V2—were actually got into production. London and southern England had their last ordeal from these unpiloted bombs in the spring and summer of 1944 and suffered considerable damage and casualties. But the

invasion of Europe came just in time to avert the worst
of these attacks. By the spring of 1945 the Russians were
hammering at Berlin while the British and the Americans
were on the Rhine and the Southern Alps. Their advance
was irresistible, and on 8th May, 1945—V.E. Day—the
German armies at last laid down their arms, leaving the
victors from east and west face to face with their own
ideological differences, so far ignored in the interests of
victory over the common enemy.

The years which have since elapsed have fallen into
two distinct periods. Victory immediately disclosed ideological differences, hitherto suppressed, which split the
victorious Allies into two armed, hostile camps, symbolised in Europe by the Iron Curtain : a physically and
spiritually impenetrable barrier cutting Germany in half
and separating Russia and her Balkan and Eastern satel-
lites from the still powerful Western powers, denounced
as Capitalist and Imperialist by enemies, but preferring
to call themselves Democratic. With the renascent and
unpredictable power of Communist China temporarily
behind her, Russia was overwhelmingly powerful in con-
ventional forces. The West relied in the last analysis on
the 'Nuclear Deterrent', in which American technologists
had gained a decisive lead. Stalemated in Europe, the
Communists turned to territorial aggression in Asia and
subversive activities in Africa, South America, and the
Middle East designed to exploit the chaos into which
German and Japanese victories had plunged all the old
colonial empires. In Malaysia, Borneo, and Kenya,
Indonesia and Cuba, Algeria and Tunisia small wars
dragged on as the newly emergent nations sought to de-
fine their frontiers and allegiances. Israel fought successfully to establish a unified state precariously surrounded
by hostile Arabs. A mixed force, in fact mainly American,
but nominally representing the United Nations' Organisation, which had replaced the defunct League of
Nations, fought a major campaign to halt the Chinese
advance in North Korea. Only now has America tenta-
tively extricated herself from another major war undertaken to save for Western democracy the Indo-Chinese

peninsula, where the French had dismally failed to hold their prosperous dependencies. The peace of 1945 has so far been illusory and remains precarious.

Most catastrophic for Britain was the disruption of the Empire. Politicians had long hoped the colonies would progressively reach the stage of education and prosperity which would qualify them to assume the responsibilities of the self-governing Dominions. Even before the War progress had already been both too fast for naturally conservative colonial officials and too slow for ambitious native politicians. In the aftermath of war the administrators were over-anxious to escape imperial financial burdens and the world-wide denunciations of 'colonialism', and the local politicians over-confident of their ability to shepherd their peoples into the patterns of Western democracy. A precipitate withdrawal from all imperial responsibility, often while war still raged, leaving frontiers still undefined and tribal rivalries still unresolved, led to much unnecessary disorder and bitter feuds, racial and religious, which time has done nothing to heal.

In India—an Empire in itself—over-hasty withdrawal amidst considerable bloodshed produced two irreconcilable states, Hindu India and Moslem Pakistan, as members of the new British Commonwealth of Nations. Meanwhile the prodigious advance of China to the status of a major nuclear power opened a new phase in world politics. The West can take some comfort from the mutual hostilities of China and Russia. But tensions in the Near, Middle, and Far East and elsewhere have also increased, so that the danger that a trivial local dispute may at any moment involve the whole world in a self-destructive major war is, if anything, greater than ever. Moreover China's conquest of Tibet and appearance in strength on the Himalayas has vastly complicated the difficulties of India and Pakistan.

Throughout the Empire experiments were launched designed to achieve similar ends, though infinitely varied in constitutional form and in their chances of success. Both progressives and traditionalists ardently believed that this compromise would fulfil the hopes of both: that a common interest in peaceful, democratic political progress, a common need for promoting prosperity by mutual aid, and the obvious advantage of pursuing a common defence policy against subversive influences designed to sabotage both these endeavours, would produce a world-wide community bound together by shared ideals, the paramount need for material progress, and a long tradition of co-operative effort. It was hoped that this new Commonwealth would find a symbol of unity in the King, whom even the Republican members recognised as 'Head of the Commonwealth', and effective direction from the annual conference of Prime Ministers.

In England itself peace by no means meant the end of the national crisis. The second World War had more or less completed the processes observable at the end of the first. In spite of generous help from the Dominions and the U.S.A., all the remaining reserves of gold and dollars and all the big holdings of foreign investments had gone to pay for the desperate resistance of the middle years of the war. Every capital need had been sacrificed to the same end, so that out-of-date machinery and mining equipment handicapped every branch of British industry in the fight for markets against the modernised, streamlined industry of America; and a mass of damaged property had to be restored or replaced as a prior charge on what slender capital resources there were. The accumulated wealth of the 19th century had gone; and the food and petrol and tobacco of this over-crowded, over-industrialised population had now to be paid for week by week by exports. Fortunately in a world so damaged, there was for a time no lack of markets for all exportable commodities, mostly paid for by the customers out of generous American aid. But even so, the British war effort had to be prolonged far into the peace, and it is significant that food and clothes and petrol had to be rationed in Britain long after such restrictions had disappeared elsewhere—even in Germany.

As with the economic trends, so with the social. In the mass warfare of 1914–18 the British people had earned political equality for themselves. The reward for their effort against Hitler was to be social security, so that all should henceforth be protected from the worst miseries of the 1930s. The wartime government had already worked out the Beveridge plan for giving every citizen some form of national insurance against sickness, unemployment, old age, and want. But men and women who had been in the armed services or who had kept industry going in spite of bombed-out factories and homes expected a more substantial reward in terms of a higher standard of living, better housing, and shorter working hours. They reckoned that they were more likely to get this from Mr Attlee than from Winston Churchill; and the Socialists gained a clear-cut victory in the immediately post-war election. Under them the lingering remnants of 19th century *lassez-faire* were swept away, and the State assumed responsibility for the welfare and security of all its citizens. It took direct control of mines and railways by nationalisation and would have done the same for road transport and the steel industry but for the narrow victory of Churchill's Conservatives in the General Election in 1951.

By 1952 there seemed to be solid grounds for hoping that the worst was over. Commercially and industrially Britain was more than holding her own in a hotly competitive post-war world. The damages of war had been largely made good and both political parties had housing programmes which promised ultimately to meet the swollen needs of a vastly over-congested population. There had been no large-scale unemployment. A huge American loan had tided over the period of industrial reconstruction, though on somewhat exorbitant terms. The Welfare State was a going concern and had relieved the poor, and, indeed, many among the professional classes, of the worst anxieties which had previously dogged them. It was an achievement by the British almost more remarkable, because more humdrum and unspectacular, than that of the war years; and the coronation of Queen Elizabeth II became largely a celebration of that achievement. The great gathering of Commonwealth representatives showed that the Crown was still working powerfully in holding together not only the British, but also the many diverse peoples of the old Empire in a single loyalty and community of interest. With the end of rationing in sight, optimists could reasonably believe that a new Elizabethan Age was about to dawn.

Today there can be few in Britain who still indulge such hopes. For a few years it did seem that the Commonwealth might, in a chaotic world, exercise a major stabilising influence, grounded on a common interest in peace and in establishing equitable standards of living, the habit of consultation and co-operation, and a shared belief in genuinely representative government. At the head of such a body Britain could have spoken with an authority among the great powers out of all proportion to her shrunken material resources. This dream was ended mainly by the nationalism, racialism, and separatism of the new African states, which became fanatical when South Africa adopted a policy of *Apartheid* wholly unacceptable to western civilisation and, in 1961, opted out of the Commonwealth altogether. The Rhodesian Federation, hopefully established in 1953, broke apart ten years later; white Rhodesia has followed the example of South Africa and so far successfully defied the economic sanctions imposed not only by Britain, but also by all members of the United Nations' Organisation. Expulsions of Asians in East Africa and persecution of British businessmen throughout the continent provide little hope that the Commonwealth Conference, even if it continues to meet, can achieve any profitable concerted action.

Within the African states themselves tribalism and economic difficulties have made democratic constitutions unworkable. Governments, in order to survive, have been led to set up one-party rule or military autocracies; and where English influence survives at all it derives from the Royal Military Academy at Sandhurst rather than the London School of Economics. The Federation of Nigeria has so far survived, but only at the price of a destructive civil war. Outside Africa the West Indies Federation disintegrated in 1962 into its component island parts, all too small to exist with safety, either economically or militarily, in the jungle of the contemporary world. India and Pakistan, though still officially members of the Commonwealth, lapsed into open war in 1961 on the vexed issue of Kashmir. Though this was prudently halted before much damage had been done, the bitter civil war in 1972 between East and West Pakistan which has resulted in the emergence of Bangladesh has brought all the old jealousies and hatreds to the surface; and peace and unity in the Indian sub-continent seem now further off than ever. Thanks to the active intervention of British armed forces, the Federation of Malaysia set up in 1963 not only survives, but also has been expanded to include Brunei, once the British part of Borneo; and the threat of communist infiltration from Indonesia has been fended off. But even there Singapore opted for independence in 1965 so as to keep for herself the large profits of her commercial activities; and the numerous Chinese population presents grave problems.

In Britain itself the years since the coronation have been almost equally disappointing. On the surface the nation's political machinery has continued to function smoothly along traditional lines. When Churchill retired in 1955 he was succeeded by Sir Anthony Eden, who duly secured a comfortable majority in the General Election which followed. But Eden was already a sick man and quite unfit to handle successfully the major crisis of 1956 in the Middle East when Egypt, provoked by a withdrawal of American aid, nationalised the Suez Canal. Israel in turn was provoked to war; and Franco-British intervention, ill conceived, ill timed, and ineptly carried out, resulted only in the total blocking of the Canal to international traffic and gravely damaged Britain's international prestige. Eden fell; but his party remained in power, still with a comfortable majority, first under Harold Macmillan and then under Sir Alec Douglas-Home, until the Socialists won the General Election of 1964.

In perspective the 1960s were a dreary period in British

political and social history. When Harold Wilson, by the narrowest of margins, won the 1964 General Election he inherited from his opponents a stagnant industry bedevilled by wildcat strikes and restrictive practices; growing inflation, as prices, wages, and public expenditure remorselessly rose; a falling balance of trade, as the nation priced itself out of the export market; and an impending currency crisis, as the world lost faith in Britain's ability to maintain the value of the pound. He set himself buoyantly to prove that Labour could provide better government, a more equitable society, and greater prosperity; and he was convincing enough to secure a more comfortable majority in a quick election in 1966. His government found the trade unions just as recalcitrant as before. The cost of living rose faster than ever; and a continuously adverse balance of trade forced yet another devaluation of the pound. Their attempt to get into the Common Market was baulked, as the Conservative effort had been before, by President de Gaulle's obstinate use of France's Veto; and the joint attempt by the Prime Minister and Barbara Castle to achieve a voluntary agreement stabilising prices and wages was rejected by the trade unions. Their downfall in 1970 was due to a profound disillusionment of the electorate, rather than to any enthusiasm for the promises offered by Ted Heath, the new and triumphant leader of the Conservatives.

But in truth this disillusionment went far deeper than a mere discontent with the performance of the Socialist government. The whole post-war trend in Britain has been towards Consensus politics : an appeal to a hypothetical middle-of-the-road voter who is presumed to sway elections. The two great parties are no longer divided by deep ideological differences. Both tend to regard material prosperity as their only goal. They are agreed on the need for more houses and for extending opportunities for secondary and higher education, particularly for the scientists and technologists required in ever increasing numbers by a modern society. Both deplore the inflation which has steadily eroded savings, pensions, and fixed incomes for more than thirty years, though neither has succeeded in checking it. Both aim at a social justice which shall prevent any section of the community feeling that it is being exploited for the benefit of others. Only on the pace and degree of reform and on the methods of achieving it do the parties differ violently.

Perhaps partly because of this, the authority and prestige of Parliament itself have noticeably diminished during this period. Its debates have presented to the public a picture of rival administrators vigorously accusing each other of incompetence, rather than that of men of high principle arguing their sincerely held beliefs. A situation is developing in which the electorate as a whole is given no opportunity of pronouncing on issues on which it feels strongly and in which its vital interests are involved. In 1970 both parties had declared for joining the Common Market if "acceptable" terms could be negotiated. But since neither would say acceptable to whom and in what terms, the voices of those who feared a widespread and inequitable rise in prices went unheard and unrepresented. Worse still, issues of high principle on which thoughtful people are deeply and sincerely worried, such as the abolition of capital punishment, easier divorce, and the legalisation of abortion are, in the modern phrase, "lifted out of the arena of party politics" and left to the free vote of the House of Commons. On such matters the opinion of the Commons cannot always be taken as the expression of the national conscience and many electors may justifiably feel that they are being virtually disfranchised.

There have been no dramatic crises as the Welfare State has gradually developed into what is called the Affluent Society which, in turn, is slowly merging into the Permissive Society : only an unforeseen and progressive loss of a sense of moral purpose, especially among the young, and an irresponsibility of behaviour which has to some extent infected all classes and all generations. The widely publicised excesses of emancipated youth—the student demonstrations, the sit-ins, and the forceful occupation of public buildings—are all proclaimed as peaceful assertions of opinion, but are all too often deliberately planned to provoke violence and to silence the voices of opponents. The motives behind such outbursts are generally pacifist and humanitarian : a horror of war, a deep desire to alleviate the world's miseries, and a longing to control the society in which they will have to live and which they feel their elders have grossly mismanaged. But they are easily exploited by left-wing agitators who wish only to dislocate the fabric of Western civilisation and create a climate of revolution. Those in authority in universities and colleges, often sympathetic to the aims of the demonstrators and guiltily conscious of the mistakes and short-coming of their own generation, have mostly adopted a policy of appeasement which satisfies neither the aspirations of the young nor the exasperated resentment of taxpayers who feel that their gift of a free education is being squandered in anti-social activity.

The less intellectual young, meanwhile, express their frustration in a society which has freed them from want by violent gang warfare, by interrupting football matches, breaking up railway carriages, or, in an access of hysteria, smashing all the shop windows in the high street of Clacton-on-Sea. Behind all is the insidious spread of the consumption of drugs, some harmless in themselves, but dangerously liable to lead to heroin addiction; and Hippies, dependent on the good will of too kindly fellow citizens, proclaim the bliss of a drug-sodden nirvana. Bewildered magistrates and police authorities have as yet found no confident answer to these phenomena; and baffled parents have to confess that the loss of their complete control of the family's purse-strings has also largely deprived them of the ability to restrain the activities of their adolescent children.

Unfortunately the performance of large sections of the adult working population during these past critical years has given them little right to protest at the irresponsibility of the young. The prevailing attitude has become that epitomised in the Sellers film : "I'm All Right Jack".

Over the whole of English society have hung the twin clouds of continuous inflation and a persistent failure to balance foreign payments. The self-discipline of the war years has been forgotten. Restrictive practices, wild-cat strikes, and an obstinate resistance to all proposals designed to make labour more productive continue to hamper industrial recovery. The more powerful trade unions and other pressure groups ruthlessly protect their members from the discomforts attendant on the con-tinuous rise in the cost of living, while those who depend on fixed incomes and occupational pensions face a pro-gressively bleaker future and people who have responded to the government's ceaseless appeals to save money are repaid only in heavily depreciated currency. It is small wonder that the nation is full of discontents and that the restored balance of trade is precariously maintained.

Such a record cannot be regarded as the birth pangs of a new Elizabethan Age. It would nevertheless be wrong to despair of Britain's future either at home or abroad. Much, clearly, has gone irretrievably wrong. Unnecessarily large tracts of attractive countryside have been obliterated by badly planned building develop-ment. Largely uncontrolled Commonwealth immigration has created an intractable problem in some industrial areas. The rise in the number of car owners has already left far behind expensive plans for the provision of safe roads and adequate parking space in an island too small for its still growing population. The attempt to halt inflation by government control of prices and incomes is breaking down. In fact it looks as though the 1970s, in contrast with the dreary 60s, will go down in political history as an extremely critical decade. The Industrial Relations Act was the most clearly defined mandate given to the government at the General Election; and were the trade unions to force a second appeal to the voters they would quite certainly find a large majority against them. But it has roused issues most people thought long since dead and has inevitably provoked that confronta-tion which Mr Heath has always professed himself anxious to avoid.

Thus there is ugly talk, reminiscent of 1921 and 1926, of industrial, rather than political, action to force the nation to accept the wishes of the more extremist union leaders; and their position is far stronger than it was in 1926. Mergers and ever closer integration have meant that large sections of industry can be brought to a halt by even a quite small strike in a single factory. The transport workers and dockers combined can bring British export trade to a standstill and dislocate the nation's daily life. Tempers have got shorter on the shop floor and strike picketing has already ceased to be in any meaningful sense peaceful; and there are no signs in 1973 that the government has made adequate preparations for a show-down with the unions such as Baldwin made in 1925. At the same time the Irish question is back with us in its most intractable form, and almost the whole of the Army's reserves have been absorbed by the effort to prevent civil war in Ulster. Unemployment figures are tending to rise. The pace of inflation, far from being "contained", has accelerated alarmingly. The balance of payments is again on the danger line; and though the pound is not for once the most immediately threatened currency unit in a world monetary crisis, it cannot be said that the financial situation is under effective control. Even the possibility of sudden, rapid, and uncontrollable inflation, such as Central Europe suffered after 1918, has ceased to be altogether an alarmist and laughable nightmare.

What is significant is that these possibilities are no longer merely fantasies of those old enough to remember earlier crises, but have begun to impinge on a wider public plagued by gas and electricity cuts, coal shortages, rising food prices, and the recurrent daily nightmare of commuting to work when one of the railway unions is working to what is called rule. Courageous and imaginative leadership could, of course, resolve all these difficulties except, almost certainly, the Irish question. If one of the great political parties cannot soon provide that leadership, it seems probable that the British electorate, in spite of its much vaunted commonsense and moderation, will begin to look left or right for some more dictatorial short cut to a world where prices are stable, savings reasonably protected, and trains run on time.

But, of course, these are the extremes of fear; and there are also plenty of hopeful signs. While extremists make all the noise most young peope are quietly learning to take advantage of the vastly extended new opportunities now available. There is increasing support for leisure activities ranging from youth orchestras to athletic clubs and volunteer rescue services for those who run into trouble on mountains or at sea; and those who organise such things report a growing enthusiasm and a ready acceptance of the necessary disciplines. In this context it is perhaps significant that the Ulster crisis which has placed the Army in a most unenviable and dangerous situation has been reflected in a remarkable improvement of its hitherto unsatisfactory recruiting figures. Sooner or later the sensible majority will prevail. Of course there will also be more mistakes. A community schooled for generations to the pursuit by each individual of his own enlightened self-interest cannot overnight accept the idea of social justice for all. Simple men do not easily grasp complex economic issues, and a fearful burden falls on scientists, economists, trade union leaders, and the politicians who have to form and guide public opinion. Britain has still to accustom herself to the fact that she will not again rule the waves nor control an empire on which the sun never sets. But, if she can put her house in order, she still has the political wisdom and maturity accumulated over the centuries to enable her to take her place in the forefront of the world's civilised nations.

Index